BUY
A MILLION
DOLLARS ®

Greco Garcia

What you and your children never learned
in school about making your money GROW

Buy a Million Dollars® –
What you and your children never learned in school
about making your money grow

ISBN 0-9755812-1-X
First edition © 2005

Cover design by Jorge Tirado

Published by T K & G Publishing

1800 Robertson Blvd. 125
Los Angeles, California 90035
(310) 827-9060
www.buyamilliondollars.com
www.compreunmillon.com

The ideas in this book are based on the author's education and accumulated experience, and they are presented with the intention of informing, entertaining and inspiring the reader.

The author and publisher believe the information presented in this book can be helpful and should be available to the public. But this book is not sold under the premise that the author and publisher are engaged in rendering legal, accounting, tax, financial planning or any other professional service, nor do the author and publisher advocate specific securities as investments (expressed or implied). This text should be used only as a general guide and not as your primary resource for making financial decisions.

Investing is not a "get-rich-quick" scheme. You must understand that accumulating wealth and becoming economically independent do not happen overnight; they happen over time. Furthermore, because there is always risk involved in financial decision-making in general and investing in particular, and because each person is different and each situation unique, the author and publisher urge you, the reader, to consult a professional financial advisor before making any financial decisions. It is a sign of wisdom and prudence to seek professional assistance.

Do not use this book if you are not willing to assume all of the risk and accept full and complete personal responsibility for your decisions, actions and results.

Neither the author nor the publisher shall have liability or responsibility to any person or entity for any injury, loss or damage caused or alleged to be caused, directly or indirectly, by any of the information in this book.

To Triana and Kostas, my children, who were my inspiration in writing this book. They are teaching me to be more consistent, to be more patient and to become a better teacher.

To my mother, Gloria, for introducing me to Christmas savings accounts at age 12.

Finally, to all the people who have been my students and are saving, buying homes and learning to buy a million dollars®.

Contents

PREFACE

After writing this book, I had the opportunity to talk with Mr. Raul Batiz, a very successful businessman from Mexico. After many years of owning and running a dynamic, international agriculture business, he is now retired and doing the things he loves.

With his lovely wife, ten children and many grandchildren, he is enjoying a stress-free life because he followed the principles that many successful people use to become financially independent.

A self-made success story, Mr. Batiz's only education was attending school through the seventh grade, as well as what he calls the "school of life."

He started to work at the age of 12, selling newspapers in the streets and cleaning offices for different businesses. Looking back, he feels that it was important for him to start to work early in life, because it builds character and teaches a person to be dependable and trustworthy.

Moving on from these early jobs, Batiz then started to work in his father's agriculture business, where he learned the trade. A few years later, he was able to buy his own farm with money he saved and a bank loan.

Batiz feels that working consistently and saving money is very important. By starting his own business, he learned that having a good working relationship with banks was a key element in his success. As he started to understand what was important to banks, he learned that financial statements were essential to the success of his business.

In 1971, one of his uncles asked Batiz to help open a

sales office in Nogales, Arizona to be able to export produce to the U.S. This provided a chance to open his own office and led him into his second business, exporting produce from Mexico. At the same time, it taught him to learn from others, become independent and take advantage of opportunities when they present themselves. At this point, Batiz needed help and called on his sons to assist him with managing and running his business, which eventually became a family business with millions of dollars in sales every year.

I asked him to share his philosophy on the following topics.

What advice would you give to young people?
Get an education, work during summer vacation as young as possible, and always save money.

How old should you be when you start to work?
I started to work when I was 12 years old, so I think children can start when they get to the seventh grade in school.

How important is it to save?
Since saving money helped me start my first business, I feel it is very important. However, it is more important to teach your children to save.

Do you invest in the stock market?
No, I never learned.

As a father, what did you find important to teach your children?
Set a good example in everything that you do.

What mistakes do you feel that your children have made with their own children?
Giving them too much and not having them work.

What advice can you give someone with children?
Teach by example.

Should someone work at a job or start a business?
First get experience by working at a job and then start your own business.

As you will see in the following pages, the principles that Mr. Batiz acquired have also helped me to achieve financial success.

INTRODUCTION

Today, I find that people are having the same money problems that I faced when I got out of college in 1979. I had a college degree. I had my first good job (or so I thought) in Los Angeles and was excited about beginning my new life as a professional person. However, nine months after starting my first job, I had a problem; I wasn't able to cover my monthly expenses.

If I was short of money every month, I knew I couldn't call home and ask my parents to send me any. I had been living better as a student than as a professional person. Today, 25 years later, I continue to meet hundreds of people with the same money problems in the United States and in the ten other countries where I do business.

I ask myself why so many people have money problems in all these places. Why aren't we taught basic money skills by our parents and in school? If money is important to all of us and we all have money problems, then why don't we learn how to avoid them?

Now, more than 30 years after graduating from high school, I feel I understand why so many people don't know the reason for their financial problems. It's because they don't learn about money management and the relationship between earning it and spending it.

Since they never learned the basics of money, they don't understand why they are in debt, why they don't have savings, and why their money doesn't grow.I see two reasons for this.

The first is that our parents don't teach us at home. Some

of our parents might have mentioned saving money, but that was about it. The reality is that they themselves were never taught the basics about money, and therefore they didn't have a plan to teach us about it.

The second is that in school we aren't taught anything about money and how to make it grow. In school, we are supposed to get good grades. That way, we can get into college, where we are supposed to get good grades in order to get a good job.

Theoretically, we want to get a good job to make a good income, but then we start to work and find out that a good income isn't enough to cover our monthly expenses. We don't understand what happened because we thought we did everything we were supposed to do.

What is a good income anyway?

We don't have any idea what a good income is when we are younger, unless we earn money while going to school. Instead, we find out when we get our first job and have to pay bills, and our income isn't enough to cover them.

I did what I was supposed to do. I got a college education to get what I thought was a good job with a good income. But after a year of working, the money that I earned wasn't enough to live well in Los Angeles.

I figured that if I could just earn an extra $500 to $700 each month, this would help me with my expenses, but to live well in Los Angeles I needed to earn at least $50,000 a year. In 1980, it wasn't easy to earn that much in the first or second year with a company, especially in the type of work I was doing. I started to look for a new job, but instead I discovered the opportunity I was looking for. I found a way to start my own business, which had a better financial future than a job. This is where my education about money and financial success began.

Between teaching myself through books, by trial and error, and through people I met who became my teachers, I started to learn about money.

I learned how to earn it, how to keep earning it and how to invest to make it grow. What I learned about money taught me to ask myself the following question – *"Am I making my money grow or am I making it disappear?"*

Million-Dollar Lessons

Let me share how I was able to do well financially. By this, I mean that I can pay all my monthly expenses without worrying, not owe any money except the mortgage, and save a substantial amount every month without a formal education in finances or accounting.

I'll show you the important rules I have learned about money. Everyone who has a hard time paying bills, owes money or doesn't have money saved for retirement needs to learn these rules to be able to make their money grow – to as much as a million dollars or more!

You don't have to learn a lot of things, just a few concepts. For me, this was the key to feeling secure and not worrying about money. I will show you how I was able to teach myself in a very simple way.

Remember, if you are having money problems, it not only affects you, it also affects your family. Even more importantly, if you don't learn about money, then how can you teach your children about it? I want this book to make you think about what you are teaching them.

You'll see how, little by little, I have taken steps to teach my children Triana (ten) and Kostas (eight) about money. I decided to show them simple rules because as a child I wasn't taught how to handle my money and make it grow. I tell them that learning a few rules about money now can make their lives a lot easier in the future.

If you owe money, if you don't take vacations, if you aren't buying a house, if you don't have any savings, well, your children don't have these things either. Whatever you have or don't have in your life will be the same in your children's lives. It's up to you.

This book will help you make changes and be more successful with the money that you earn. If you have financial problems, these changes might not seem to be what you need to fix your problems. They might not make sense because you want to see immediate results and only winning the lottery can solve that.

The key is not how you are doing financially today; the key is how you will be financially at 60 years old. Someone once told me, "Success is not a sprint race; success is a marathon." Making your money grow takes time, consistency and patience. In the U.S. and Canada, you can buy a house in payments, you can buy a car in payments – and you can also buy a million dollars in payments! I'll show you how!

As I a write this book, I'm buying a house in payments. The house cost $800,000 and is now worth more. The loan amount is $600,000 at 5 percent interest and my payment is around $3,220 per month. By the time I pay off the house (my goal is eight years) it will be worth more than a million dollars.

Let's suppose that when you are 20 years old, you start to save and invest $100 a month at 10 percent interest. By the time you are 60 – 40 years later – you'd have $632,408 and, with wise investing this could be a $1,000,000. If you started at the age of 30, you would have to save and invest $500 to have those million dollars.

In both examples, you are buying a million dollars with less money per month than I am buying a million-dollar house with, right?

In this book, you'll learn "How to buy a Million Dollars®." Let's get started.

PART ONE

1. LEARN TO EARN MONEY

"A job is just an activity that you do to generate money." Greco Garcia.

We earn money by what we call work, but I call this an activity.

While I was growing up, I always had an activity to make money. I remember selling used comic books, mowing lawns, washing cars and selling newspapers on the street. I also took care of the plants for two families and worked as a lifeguard in the summer.

While I was in high school, I played sports and had two jobs. One was drafting for a teacher at his house for $1.75 an hour. I really liked that job because of the experience, but learning to draw plans for homes that were actually built was even more exciting.

After a year of working with him, I went off on my own and started a drafting business. I was able to draw the plans for ten homes that were built in 1974 and are still standing today.

The other job I had in high school was working as a bellboy at a local hotel. I got the job after a friend of mine told me he was quitting. He said he was paid $1.35 an hour, plus tips. When I asked how much he was making in tips, I was totally surprised to hear he was making $30 to $40 a day. That was much more than most of my friends were making at that time. I didn't think twice about it – he recommended me and I immediately started working as a bellboy.

At that point, I learned a valuable lesson that has served

me well over the years. I could have one activity; and at the same time, earn two or three incomes. I guess that was – and still is – one of the secrets of the rich. *One activity that brings in two or three incomes!*

Today I realize how every job I had when I was young was important. With each, I always looked for new ways to earn money until I found something better. And I learned never to complain about the jobs that I had.

I learned about earning money, how to account for it, save it, take care of it. And I learned about banks and interest.

Since I began working at an early age, I see the benefits when children start working early. I always ask parents what the right age is for their children to start to work. I get answers like, "15 years old," "at the age of 18" and "after they get out of school." There is really no one right answer, but I tell them, *the earlier the better!*

Remember, children do chores, but you don't pay them. Instead you get them things that they need, and some of you do it in the form of an allowance. However, look at it – *children do everyday jobs or activities to get compensated by their parents. They do things for you when they really want something or want permission from you.*

Then you say something like this – *"If you mow the lawn, I will let you...."* You see, they have to carry out an activity in order for you to give them something. They have to fulfill their responsibilities. I see this as work. I'd like to share some ideas of how to earn money, so that you can teach them to your children. In turn, these exercises can help you discover how to *increase your own earning power.*

Teach Your Children to Earn Money

This is what I've done to prepare my children for the world of earning money. Before I started to talk to Triana and Kostas about money, I taught them about responsibilities.

First they learned personal responsibilities, like brushing their teeth and taking a bath before bed. Then they took on family tasks, such as picking up their plates from the table after dinner and taking out the trash. They learned to do their homework as soon as they got home from school, and so on.

When they didn't want to carry out their responsibilities, this is what I told them, *"If you don't do your part, I won't do my part."* If they wanted something, I'd ask them, *"Have you done your part?"* If not, I would ask, *"If I don't do my work, do you think I'll get paid?"* "No," they'd reply.

At that point I knew they realized that if they wanted something from me, they needed to do their part by fulfilling their responsibilities. They understood the relationship between working and receiving compensation for it. I think the first lesson we need to learn is about responsibility.

When I was a boy, I was given an allowance for doing my chores and Triana and Kostas also learned to carry out their responsibilities at home, so they could earn an allowance. It was usually $10 and they would receive it on Sundays. This was their first experience in generating income.

Then their mother showed them how to run a lemonade stand. They learned a lot about business. She taught them to prepare the lemonade, how to sell it, how to make change, and how to put in the necessary time to sell their product. They also learned that the money they made depended on how much lemonade they sold.

Next, they put on a yard sale, which was much like the lemonade stand. But they also learned that there are many different things they can sell. Again they practiced dealing with people, setting prices and making change, and they saw the results of the hours worked. But to me, the most important lesson from these activities was learning to sell.

My children then discovered that a business is better than a job by starting their own business – *recycling plastic bottles and aluminum cans.*

Triana and Kostas learned that they could get five cents for each can and plastic bottle they turned in, although they didn't know how much they'd make. They asked me to save my empty water bottles instead of throwing them away, and this is how they got started.

When we took the cans and bottles to the recycling center for the first time, they got their receipt from the recycling machine and went next door to the grocery store to exchange it for money. They were very excited when they each got about $7.00.

At that point, I asked them a very important question. "Who else can you ask to save you their empty cans and bottles?" They asked our neighbor, Sylvia. With the bottles that Sylvia and I saved, each child got $14.00 on the second trip to the recycling center. This time, they were even more excited.

They learned two things from the recycling business. First, they were doing one activity to earn money, but got two people to do it for them – *one activity, two incomes.* Second, they learned that they could make more money in less time than with the lemonade stand and the yard sale.

I told Triana and Kostas how in high school I worked as a bellboy and got paid both by the hour and in tips. I taught them *"one activity with two incomes is better than a job with one income."* However, it is also important that they work at a regular job that pays by the hour, so they can see the difference between a job and a business.

Get an Insider's View

One day Triana asked me what an interior designer does, because that is what our neighbor, Ellen, does for a living. My daughter wanted to find out a little more about this work, so I suggested that she ask if she could go to work with Ellen one day. Ellen was pleased with my little girl's interest and they set a date when there was no school. I told Triana to ask Ellen questions about her work and what she does.

As it turned out, Triana was gone all day. When she

returned, you could see the excitement on her face. She was glad she went and told me she'd learned that interior designers help people with their homes. They don't stay in the office all day, but go to stores to shop for furniture. They visited the Pacific Design Center in Los Angeles and Triana also found out how much interior designers earn per hour.

I hope you can imagine what kind of experience this was for Triana and what she discovered in just one day. As we know, not everything is learned in school, so this is another way of finding out about earning money in the real world. If your children have the opportunity to go to work with relatives or friends for a day, they'll get firsthand experience of how other people work and the type of work they do.

You, too, can ask others what they like and don't like about their jobs. This will give you different ideas about how others work and let you compare your job to theirs. *All this will help you discover the best activity to increase your income!*

Working for Yourself Vs. Working for Others

If you have a job, you are working for someone else. *If you work for someone else, that person controls your income. In turn, this dictates where you live, if you take vacations, and the time you spend with your family. Most importantly, you are limited on how much money you can make.* When you work for yourself, *you* are the one in control.

Taxes are the reason you don't take home more money each month. And if you work for someone else, you pay more taxes. When you work for yourself, you pay less in taxes because you have more tax deductions. So how do you lower your taxes and earn more money? Have a home-based business. It will give you a second income *and* more tax deductions.

Through a home-based business you will learn sales, which is one of the best ways to earn more money without having a boss or a schedule. *When things are going well for you at work, that is the ideal time to start something of your own on a part-time basis. This can eventually turn into a full-time income.*

In December of 1980, I started a home-based business with Herbalife International on a part-time basis. Four months later, it turned into a full-time business. I've found that *the best thing about Herbalife is the success-training program that they have.* Today, my business grosses more than $12,000,000 in sales per year and I still handle everything from my home office with no employees. So I recommend that you look into starting a home-based business for three reasons: you gain an additional income; you pay less in taxes; and you can achieve freedom from your job, as you will see in Chapter Four.

When Triana and Kostas were born, I was always at home and was able to take them to school and pick them up. As they grew up, they knew I was always there for them. They never saw me hold a job. *Do you think I want my children to have a job when they grow up or do you think I want them to be independent and have a business?*

I will encourage them to work at different jobs so they can understand the difference between hours worked, the amount of money they make, and what they can buy with the money they earn. However, ultimately I will recommend that Triana and Kostas have a business and not a job, because this is what I have done.

2. HOW MUCH MONEY WILL YOU EARN?

One of the things we don't learn in school is how many years we will work during our careers. We never calculate how much money we'll earn and how much money we'll save by the time we retire.

Most people start to work around the age of 20 or 25 and retire at around 60 or 65 years of age. But how much money will they have earned and how much will they have saved by the time they retire?

The average person works around 40 to 45 years of his or her life, and that means we have only a limited number of years to work, just like an athlete.

A professional athlete plays between 8 to 15 years, depending on the sport. When he retires from sports at an early age, an athlete wants to have earned as much as possible and to have saved for retirement. Otherwise, he will have a hard time supporting himself and his family after he retires.

Whether we have a job or whether we play professional sports, we have no idea how much money will pass through our hands. If we knew, we would treat our jobs and money differently.

The following table gives an idea of how much money will go through your hands in a lifetime, depending on how much you make per month and how many years you work.

If you earn $4,000 per month, you will earn $1,920,000

Earnings in				
1 Month	10 Years	20 Years	30 Years	40 Years
1,000	120,000	240,000	360,000	480,000
1,500	180,000	360,000	540,000	720,000
2,000	240,000	480,000	720,000	960,000
2,500	300,000	600,000	900,000	1,200,000
3,000	360,000	720,000	1,080,000	1,440,000
3,500	420,000	840,000	1,260,000	1,680,000
4,000	480,000	960,000	1,440,000	1,920,000
4,500	540,000	1,080,000	1,620,000	2,160,000
5,000	600,000	1,200,000	1,800,000	2,400,000
5,500	660,000	1,320,000	1,980,000	2,640,000
6,000	720,000	1,440,000	2,160,000	2,880,000
6,500	780,000	1,560,000	2,340,000	3,120,000
7,000	840,000	1,680,000	2,520,000	3,360,000

in 40 years. If you save 10 percent, you will have $192,000 by the time you turn 60 years old. This $192,000 will end up being much more money because it will grow with the help of compound interest, as you will see later.

Now that you have an idea of how much money you'll earn in a lifetime, *it's very important to choose the right line of work, so you can make as much as possible in the years that you will be working.*

You need to concentrate on how much you earn every month at your present job, but more importantly, look for a new activity (a business) to earn more money. You probably feel that if you earn more, you'll be able to have more things you want. But my experience tells me that people will spend more when they make more and not save any money.

I feel that we first should concentrate on choosing the right line of work that will give us the capability of making as much money as possible. At the same time, we need to save for our retirement.

What is the Best Activity to Earn Money?

After 24 years of dealing with all different types of people, I feel that *the best activity to earn money is a personal business.*

I learned that nine out of ten people who work at a job for a living are not happy with what they do. These people complain to me about not earning enough money, about having a tough schedule, a bad work environment, no vacations, and not having enough time with their children and family.

I have come to the conclusion that a business is the best line of work. Even though it isn't right for everybody, it has been for me. *I like the fact that I choose my schedule and don't have to commute. Since I work from home, my children see me all the time. I set an example for them and I do not have a limit on the income I make. Of course, the tax benefits are great. But more importantly – I obtain four incomes doing the same work!*

Kostas told me two weeks after starting fourth grade that the children would be able to go to work with their fathers for a day. Then he said, *"Papa, since I know where and how you work, can we go to the beach and surf instead?"*

This has worked very well for me, so my advice to you is to *start a home-based business on a part-time basis.* You can start in the evenings and on weekends until you are able to do it full time.

That's how I started my home-based business with Herbalife International. At first I worked in the evenings and on weekends, and four months later I went on to do it full-time. Today, more than 24 years later, my children and I see the benefits of a home-based business.

In the next chapter, I'll show you how people get into trouble with money.

3. DON'T GET INTO DEBT, AND IF YOU HAVE DEBT, GET OUT!

Most people I talk to owe money. It's either bad debt or good debt. The problem occurs when people owe too much money and they don't have a clue as to how much they owe. They just don't want to know.

They get into debt very slowly without noticing it and they accelerate their debt by ignoring it. They do so through an accumulation of expenses, by not taking care of their money and by choice. Excess spending not only gets us into debt. It also keeps us from accumulating money and eventually leads us to financial ruin – bankruptcy.

For people who know how much they owe, the problem is that *they don't know how many years it will take them to pay off their debts and how much it will cost them in interest over the years.* Some, whose debt is out of control, will *consolidate their loans, stop paying them or go into bankruptcy.* Whatever choice they make, this is a problem that a lot of people are facing today all over the world.

When students graduate from college in the U.S., they already have a credit card and owe about $3,000 to $7,000. In Canada, graduates usually owe between $8,000 and $12,000 Canadian dollars on their credit cards. And the problem is that young people are not taught by their parents or teachers what happens when you owe money.

They don't understand how interest works either in your favor or against you. They don't know how much it's going to cost to pay for the things they are buying. They don't know that when you owe money, it affects you every day in different ways. You have more stress, you don't feel like doing anything and you're tired all the time. This affects your family and your standard of living.

Having a good credit rating can work in your favor or work against you when you are trying to buy a million dollars®. Here's some good advice – protect your credit by paying your bills on time and by not owing money.

Credit Cards

The main reason people get into debt is by using credit cards and not being able to pay them off every month. Many people don't keep track of how much they charge every month, and then when the bill comes, they aren't able to pay it off completely. This is how a balance accumulates. When a balance accumulates, the interest alone makes your debt grow.

Credit card spending is the equivalent of sabotage to your family finances.

The problem is that whatever you bought with a credit card usually goes down in value, instead of going up in value. In addition, compound interest is working against you and the balances grow very rapidly. By the time people notice what is happening, their balances average from $7,000 to $14,000 in credit card debt.

Let me show you how credit card debt can work against you. In the next example, you only make the monthly payment and your debt doubles in 3.78 years because of *compound interest:*

Credit Card Balance	Interest	Doubles	Years
$5,000	19%	$10,000	3.78

On the other hand, let's see what happens to your money if you have a savings account. Your money doubles in 14.4

very slow years:

Savings Amount	Interest	Doubles	Years
$5,000	5%	$10,000	14.4

Two things happen in the above example. First, you pay 19 percent interest *(against you)* to the credit card company – a lot of interest compared to what you can earn in a savings account. Second, you are only getting 5 percent interest *(in your favor)* from the bank, and your money is growing very slowly as your debt grows much faster.

Here's another example of how compound interest can work against you. Let's say you have a $1,000 balance on a credit card at 19 percent interest. If you pay only the monthly minimum, *it will take you 19 years to pay off the $1,000.00.*

My advice is to keep track of how much you charge on your credit cards every day, and pay that amount plus the interest charge completely at the end of each month. Carry only one credit card that you can use or, better yet, use a debit card. Go to www.credit-card-direct.com on the Internet. There you can find out more about credit cards and debt.

Is It Good to Have Debt?

For me, the answer is yes. But *only* if the debt benefits you, like a loan to pay for a college education or to buy a house. This type of debt will benefit you in the future. The house will grow in value and you will pay off the loan. The college education will be valuable to you by giving you the ability to earn more money.

On the other hand, *debt is bad if you buy things like vacations, clothes and dinner at restaurants, because these things lose their value.* Always ask yourself, *"Is my money growing in value or is it decreasing in value?"*

How to Pay Your Debt

The problem is not the money that you owe. The problem is that it is very hard to pay off your debt. I'm going to show you a very simple way of repaying the money that you owe. *You have to follow the instructions or it isn't going to work for you.*

First, you need an extra dollar amount every month that will help you to pay off your debt faster. You need a minimum of $100 per month, but it can be $125, $175, $225, or $245. Whatever you decide is up to you, but it must be at least $100.

Second, you cannot use your credit cards while you are trying to pay off your debt. This will defeat your purpose. To make sure you don't use them, freeze them. Put them in a jar filled with water, cover it, put it in the freezer – and *your credit cards will be frozen*. This way you will not be tempted to use them.

To start, write down all your debts just like the example that follows:

	Debt	Monthly Payment	Duration of Payments
Credit Card 1	$3,300	$175	18.85 months
Department Store	$2,700	$125	21.60
Car	$9,000	$275	32.72
	$15,000		73.17 months
	Years to pay = 6.09 years		

As you can see, it will take you 73.17 months or 6.09 years to pay the $15,000 that is owed. Now let's say that the person above chooses to *give an extra $155* every month toward paying off the debt.

Here's what you do. Decide which debt you want to pay off first. I suggest you choose the debt with the highest rate of interest. In this example, we'll assume all three have the same interest rate, so we'll choose the one that takes the fewest months to pay off. This is credit card one with 18.85 months, followed by the department store card, while the third is the car loan.

Now you would make the following month's payment of $175 + $155 = $330 to credit card one, while you continue to make the same payments as usual on the department store charge card and the car loan.

The credit card with a $3,300 balance has a new payment of $330; thus it will take ten months to pay it off instead of 18.85 months. Once you have paid off the credit card (ten months later), you now add those $330 to the department store payment. So $125 + $330 = $455, and this is your new payment.

The department store has a balance of $2,700 and a new payment of $455; it will take 5.93 months to pay off instead of 21.60 months. Once you have paid off the department store charge card, you now add the $455 to the car payment. So $275 + 455 = $730, and this is your new payment on the car loan.

The car balance is $9,000. With a new payment of $730, it will take 12.32 months to pay off instead of 32.72 months. Take a look how much less time it would now take for you to pay off your debts.

New Debt	Amount	Monthly Payment	Duration of Payments
Credit Card 1	$3,300	$330	10 months
Department Store	$2,700	$455	5.93 months
Car	$9,000	$730	12.32 months
	$15,000		28.25 months
	Years to pay = 2.35 years		

Now you can see the difference. It will take you 28.25 months or 2.35 years to pay off the $15,000 that you owe instead of 6.09 years in the first example. Because you can pay it off in 2.35 years, you will realize a difference of 3.7 years in savings.

Remember the following rules
1. Stop using your credit cards.
2. Decide on the extra dollar amount to add to your payments. It has to be a minimum of $100.
3. Continue to make the other monthly payments.
4. Be patient.
5. If you think it's applicable, consolidate your debt.

Remember, your goal is to be able to *buy a million dollars®*. So it is very important to pay off all of your debt as soon as possible, because the interest on the debt will make it impossible for you to be able to make your money grow.

Two People Who Were Tired of Debt

Martha and her husband, friends of mine from Mexico living in Chicago, got into $40,000 in credit card debt without realizing it. They came to a seminar where I shared the steps that you are learning here and it took them eight months to implement them because they do not speak English.

In about one year and two months, they were able to pay off the $40,000 debt and saved $26,000 for a down payment on a house with a price of $260,000.

Another friend of mine, Edgar, was living in Los Angeles on $1,000 a month. He was in debt and had no savings, and he asked me for help. He began to implement the same steps that Martha did and *in two years he paid off his debt. In four years, he was able to save enough for a down payment on a $400,000 house.*

The hardest part of getting out of debt is to start. The longer it takes you to begin, the longer it will take you to lower your stress and become free of debt. Time won't stop and wait for you. Don't neglect your dream to buy a million dollars®. Make the decision today – it can change your financial future.

In the next chapter, you'll learn the first step.

4. WORK FOR YOUR SAVINGS ACCOUNT

When they go to work, most people think that they are working for themselves. The reality is that they work for somebody else. *Your work is just an activity that generates money for you.* That's true, but at the same time, you work for the government and for everybody else to whom you pay bills.

When you earn money, you first pay taxes, which are deducted from your salary. *The average American pays about 40 percent of his or her total income in taxes per year. The average Canadian pays about 45%.*

If you are lucky to have more deductible expenses, then the Internal Revenue Service (IRS) or the Canada Customs and Revenue Agency (CCRV) returns money to you at the end of the year and you are happy to receive it. The government is saving part of your money for up to a year *without paying interest on the money they return to you.* You are working for the government.

You also work to pay rent, food, utilities, phone, car, insurance, cable, Internet, vacations, clothes, etc. *Who do you really work for?* If you do not make a payment to your savings account every month and have money left over, then you are *working to pay others.*

If you do not have money left over at the end of the month, *you are working for free. If you do not have any savings, you are working for free. If you are not paying for a house, you are working for free.*

Who should you really work for? I've been working for my *savings account* and I think you should start to work for yours.

How would you feel if on Monday morning I deposited $50,000 in a savings account in your name?

Start saving 10 percent of what you earn and make it a goal to have $100,000 saved. It will do a lot for your well-being. The more you save, the better you'll feel – you'll have less stress and more self-confidence.

We all live with monthly expenses. That monthly dollar amount can be $2,500, $3,300 or $5,000 – we all have a different number we have to reach every month. We need to earn at least that much so we don't get into trouble.

Look at the example below. It isn't a complete list of the expenses you might have, but it includes the ones most of us have. Let's say your expenses are $3,500 per month. It would look like this:

Monthly Expenses	
Rent	$1,000
Food	$ 400
Car Payment	$ 350
Insurance	$ 150
Utilities	$ 100
Telephone	$ 100
Gasoline	$ 200
Others	$1,200
Total	**$3,500**

Notice there was no category for savings. That's one of the reasons you don't save any money. You are paying everybody else, except your savings account. You make sure to pay everyone on your list but, since a savings category isn't on your list, you don't pay anything toward it. *Start treating your savings account like any other expense and make sure to make that payment first every month.*

I recommend that people save 10 percent of what they

earn every month. They tell me they want to but... "I can't," "I don't have enough money at the end of the month," or "I don't make enough." If you want to, then why don't you save?

I feel that the reason people do not save is because they don't have to save.

If you don't pay one of your expenses one month, like the telephone company, they disconnect the service and you feel a negative effect immediately. If you don't pay your electric bill, the electric company disconnects the lights and you get a negative effect immediately.

If you don't pay your savings account one month, apparently nothing negative happens, right?

The Long-Term Effect

Nothing happens immediately, but *you will not have any money saved by the time you are 60 years old.*

If you don't save every month, *nothing negative happens right away.* That is the difference between saving every month and not saving every month. Just because you don't notice the consequences right away doesn't mean it will not affect you in the end.

Think about this for a moment. What will you do when you are 60 and don't have any savings? Who will take care of you? Who will you blame? *Make sure that you start to save every month.*

Another good piece of advice is to pay yourself 10 percent of everything you make. *Work for your savings account.* In 1974, I read *The Richest Man in Babylon* by George Clason, and it turned out to be one of my best lessons about money. I recommend it to everybody. Make sure you read it three times. When I read the book, I was already saving money, but after reading it, *I saved with a purpose in mind.*

The main thing to remember is *not to save in order to buy things that lose value,* but to save as much money as possible for when you retire. *If you take care of your money now and save it, then your money will take care of you in the future.*

Let me show you an example of what saving consistently, with time on your side, can do for your money. Let's say that at the age of 20, you start to save $100 per month at 10 percent annual interest.

Amount	5 years	10 years	20 years	30 years
$100	7,744	20,484	75,937	226,049
$500	38,719	102,422	379,684	1,130,244
$1600	123,899	327,752	1,214,990	$3,616,781

In 30 years, you would have $226,049, but if you continue to save the $100 until you are 60, it would become *one million dollars!* It would take you 40 years to become a millionaire, but you would do it by saving only $100 per month. *That's a very inexpensive way to buy a million dollars®.*

The reason you and your children want to start saving as soon as possible is because the monthly "payment" is less and time is on your side. Take a look at the table below:

Start to Save at Age	Save per Month	Years Saving	Amount Saved
20	$100	40	$632,408
30	$500	30	1,130,244
40	1,600	20	1,214,990
50	5,000	10	1,024,225

From this example, you can see that you can have *one million dollars* by saving and investing every month. *The earlier you start,* the *less money it costs you* per month. The later in life you begin, the more money it will cost you per month. Start to save early!

Imagine if your parents and schoolteachers had shown you the example above before you graduated from high school. How much money would you have saved with just $100 per month? Why didn't we do that? Why didn't someone tell us to do it?

We don't start to save, because the people educating us don't save and they do not teach us its importance.

You have to start to save money as soon as possible because if you don't do it, will your children save? The key is this – *if you're not saving money, they probably aren't saving either.* Remember, the best teachers children have are their parents. *Be careful what kind of example you are setting.*

I recommend that you visit the following websites. They can help you estimate how much your money can grow by the time you are 60 years old.

www.smartmoney.com

www.money.com

www.vanguard.com

Use their website calculators on saving and investing, so you can begin to see that it's a lot easier than you thought to buy a million dollars®.

Remember the following:

1. Save 10 percent of your income every month.
2. Work for your savings account, not for others.
3. By saving, you are buying a million dollars®.
4. The earlier you start to save, the better.
5. Start teaching your children to save.
6. Learn to have discipline and patience.
7. Have a long-term vision.
8. Learn how compound interest can help.

Triana Started Saving

I started to teach Triana about saving when she was four years old by getting her a piggy bank for Christmas. Every day, I gave her the loose change I had in my pockets and I'd tell her it was food for the piggy. I also started to give her a one-dollar bill every day so she could feed the bank.

My goal was for her to have $100. We could then go to a bank and open a savings account so she could have the experience of saving. It took about six weeks to save the $100. Then I suggested we go to the bank and open her own account "just like daddy." When the day arrived, she was very excited to experience the same thing as her father. I know she didn't understand the whole process, but that wasn't the point. The point was to get her into a habit of saving. It's easier to teach children when they are younger, because they are excited about learning new things.

Today Triana doesn't have a savings account in the bank; she has an investment account with Dodge and Cox. Her savings are invested in mutual funds, and every month she sees how her money is growing by learning how to follow her funds on the Internet.

The sooner you start to teach your children to save, the better. But if you don't save, then you can't teach them.

Savings Exercise

Start to save $1.00 dollar a day, and you'll have $30.00 at the end of the month. The second month, start saving $2.00 a day; you'll have $60.00 at the end of the month. Keep doing this until you form a habit.

Save per Day		
Save Per Day	Days Saved	Amount Saved at End of Month
$1.00	30	$ 30.00
$2.00	30	60.00
$5.00	30	150.00

Save per Month		
Save Per Month	Months Saved	Amount Saved at End of Year
$ 30.00	12	$ 360.00
$ 60.00	12	720.00
$150.00	12	1, 800.00

The object of this exercise is for you to *start a habit. It's difficult*, but if you start to make more money and don't learn this lesson, *you will continue to spend more than you make and not save any money.*

My experience shows me that people will spend more money if they make more money. The more they make, the more they spend. They don't save because they aren't taught early in life the importance of saving. However, they have been taught to spend.

I know what it feels like to wake up at three in the morning because I didn't know where I was going to get the money to pay my bills. It's an awful feeling. This is why I always tell people that they need to save 10 percent of what they make every month.

The Richest Man in Babylon explains the relationship of time with how money grows. The longer it takes you to start to save, the harder it is for you to accumulate money.

It is vital to understand that *it isn't how much money you earn, but how much money you keep* that will make the difference over time.

Go to the web sites listed above and use their calculators to play "what if." This will motivate you to save more consistently every month. If you do this exercise, you can better plan how much money you'll have saved when you are 60 years old.

Reasons why you should save:
1. To pay yourself first
2. To buy things that increase in value

3. To feel secure about money.
4. To have money when you turn 60 years old
5. To be able to buy a million dollars®
6. When it comes to money, it's the future that counts!

Save to Give More

Another reason we should save is to be able to help people who don't have what we have. The more prosperous we are, the more we are able to help others who are less fortunate.

As we start to save, our savings account makes us feel better and more privileged; in turn this will help us to help others. You can start by giving to your church or your favorite charity. I donate through the company where I do business, and I also give to an organization that assists the homeless.

I've learned that the better we do with our money, the better we can help others in need. If you follow the advice in this book, you'll become successful at saving and understand what I am sharing with you.

So far, you are learning the basics about money that took me a long time to understand. These will help you get out of the trouble you may be in with your finances. In the next chapter, you'll begin to understand what happens to your money every month and why it disappears.

5. HOW DID MY
MONEY DISAPPEAR?

When I got out of college and landed my first job in San Francisco, I was very excited about being a professional person and having my first job. The problem was that I wasn't earning enough money. After taxes, I was taking home approximately $800 a month. For the money that I was earning to last, I had to account for it. I had to know what I was going to spend it on, because if I ran short I knew my parents were not going to send me any.

I had to make a budget that would work for me and I still remember it. I was saving $80 per month (10 percent of the $800 I was earning) and was allowing myself to spend $17 a week for entertainment. Can you imagine having fun in San Francisco on $17 a week?

If I didn't take control of my expenses, I'd be stressed out. I really don't remember where I learned to manage my money, but I think it started when I sold newspapers as a young boy. At the end of the day, I would separate the cost of the newspapers from the profit. I couldn't spend the cost of the newspapers or I wouldn't be able to buy any to sell the following day. I had to account for the money every single day.

Earning my own money helped me learn to manage it and I also learned to save part of my income. After reading *The Richest Man in Babylon,* my savings came to be at least 10 percent of what I earned, as I discovered the secrets of how money grows.

One of the main reasons people have economic problems is that they don't have any money left over at the end of the month. Some people spend the money before the month is over and they don't have a clue about what happened to the money they earned. You cannot have control of your money if you don't know where it goes.

Public companies in the stock market have to account for their money every three months. They have to report their earnings. If they don't, they run into legal problems.

But neither our parents nor our schools teach us to account for our money on a regular basis. We don't learn how to handle it early in our lives. And we don't have a plan to control and make our money grow. We were never taught how to make a budget, and this is why many people have so much trouble with their money.

When do you think we need to understand budgets? How old should we be to learn about them? Who should teach us its use? Do you think it's important to have a budget?

I feel it is essential to learn about budgets at an early age. Something I recommend is that you show your children your monthly budget. This way, they will have an idea what your expenses are every month. If you do this with them, as I do with my children, you can help them appreciate how much things cost. You may not think this is a good idea because you might not want to show your children your money problems. If this is the case, then teach them what a budget is with the examples I showed you.

I know that if I show Triana and Kostas my monthly expenses, it can only help them in the future to handle their own money.

Your children need to start to learn the relationship between earning money and the cost of living. If they have no idea what your expenses are, they aren't able to understand how much money it takes to sustain a family. They won't understand how much they will need to earn to enjoy the same standard of living you provide for them. When you show your children your expenses, you'll see a difference in them when they ask you for things.

If my parents had just sat me down and explained each and every bill they had to pay each month and what they did to pay them, I would have had a better understanding of money at an earlier age.

You cannot teach your children what you do not know. And you can best teach your children by setting an example.

Money Coming In, Money Going Out

Every month you have money coming in – what you earn – and money going out – what you spend. If you spend more than you earn, you have problems. If you have more coming in than going out, you are in good shape.

Person	A	B	C
Earns	$1000	$ 1000	$10,000
Spends	$ -950	$-1100	$-12,000
Total	$ 50	$ -100	$ -2,000

In the previous example, person A is in a better economic situation than B and C. He has money left over, while B and C are digging a financial hole. They are starting to owe money and may even borrow money later on to be able to pay for their debt.

A teacher of mine outside of school once told me, "It's not how much money you make, it's how much money you spend." But I say, "It's not how much money you make, it's how much money you keep!"

My uncle used to say, "Greco, people get into trouble with money because they earn $1 and they spend $1.20." They should spend 90 cents and save 10 cents out of every dollar they bring in!

So what can you do to keep more money every month and stay out of trouble? Do what a business or a corporation does. Keep track of the money that you spend. *Make a budget.*

Make a Budget

When I was trying to teach my daughter what a budget is, this is what I told her. "Triana, a budget is how much money a father makes every month at his work and how much the family spends every month." I went on, "If there is money left over every month, the family can go on vacation. But if there isn't, the family won't be able to take a vacation."

She was trying to understand, so I showed her a budget based on my expenses and this is how it looked:

Rent	1100		_Jobs_
Utilites	120		doctor
telephone	350		engenier
cell	80		financial planner
car	650		arcitect
insurance	187		dentist
gas	250		
food	400		
healthinsurance	270		
Lupe	1000		
internet	50		
satalite	50		
herbalife	100		
mission	50		
club	60		
termin	38		
phone	100		

$$\$ 5455 \times 12 = \$ 65,460$$
$$\text{TEACHER } 40,000$$
$$\$ 25,460$$
$$\div \quad 12$$
$$2121.6666$$

I showed my daughter my own monthly expenses, emphasizing that our annual costs totaled $65,460. I explained that her schoolteacher earned $40,000 a year, and that she would need $2,121.66 a month more than that just to maintain our lifestyle.

Triana immediately drew a line on the page and wrote "Jobs" at the top of the new column. "Daddy, what jobs pay $65,000 a year?" she asked. I said a doctor, engineer, financial advisor, architect or dentist could earn that much. This is what she has written on the right hand side of her budget.

Imagine! She was ten years old and made this observation. What are you teaching your children about money?

A Model Budget

A budget is a tool that will tell you if you are spending too much money every month (you have problems) or if you have any left over by the end of the month (you're doing well). What follows is a very *simple one,* one that I use every month:

EARNINGS (money coming in)
Salary	$
Commissions	$
Interest	$
Total	$

EXPENSES (money going out)
Savings 10%	$
House Payment	$
Utilities	$
Car Payment	$
Insurance	$
Food	$
Telephone	$
Child Care	$
Entertainment	$
Miscellaneous	$
Etc.	$
Total	$

Subtract the *total expenses* from *total earnings*. This will tell you if you are spending too much.

Total Earnings	$ 1,100
Total Expenses	$ 1,000
Total	$ 100 (in good shape)

Total Earnings	$ 1,100
Total Expenses	$ 1,200
Total	$ -100 (in bad shape)

As you can see, this budget is very simple. You would probably add other categories and in this way, *make it your own budget.* Let me show you two different budgets – one where the person is short of money every month and another one that has money left over.

PERSON	A	B
EARNINGS	$3,600	$2,650
EXPENSES	$4,000	$2,450
TOTAL	$ -400	$ +200 (better)

As you can see, the person in example B is better off because he has $200 left over at the end of the month. *If you save $200 per month at 10 percent interest, in 30 years you would have $452,098.*

The "No Budget" Blues

Caul is 18 years old and is the son of a friend of mine who lives in San Diego. He is in his last year of high school and finally got his first job working at a car wash. He was excited to earn his own money and happy with the income he was making each month.

He started his job in the summer and was working about 112 hours per month, which gave him an income of about $832.00.

Soon after that, he decided to buy his first car. Like all of us, he was excited. He wanted a Mini Cooper, but eventually decided on a Mustang and this is what happened to his finances:

	Money earned during the summer	Money earned during the school year
Income	$832.00	$492.00
Expenses		
Car payment Insurance Gasoline	$289.00 $170.00 $ 81.00	$289.00 $170.00 $ 81.00
Total	$540.00	$540.00 **(problems)**

When Caul decided to buy the car, he was working longer hours and making more money. He didn't take into consideration that he would work less when he was back in school. As you can see, once he started school, he began to notice that he was earning less and no longer had any money left over at the end of the month.

What would happen if he had more fixed expenses than just the car? *This* is how we start to have money problems.

I asked Caul, "Who are you working for?" "The car," he replied. He got into a predicament with his money, just like a lot of people do. When Caul purchased the car, he thought he was making enough money. He made an emotional decision without considering that he would earn less once he started back to school. *Since he didn't have a budget, he began to spend more money than he earned.*

The good thing is that Caul is still 18 years old and has a lot of time to learn what I am sharing with you in this book. I hope he learned a lesson from this experience.

Understanding a Budget

What about you? How is your money situation at the end of the month? Do you have any left over, or do you come up short?

Believe me, you will continue having money problems if you don't understand that a budget can help you. A budget is a very useful tool for managing money. When you put it into action, your problems will start to disappear.

I shared with you that when I got my first job in San Francisco, I had a budget that allowed me to save $80 every month and to spend $17 a week for entertainment. My income was only $800 per month after taxes and if I was able to live with a budget on an $800 income each month, I'm sure you can live on yours!

Maybe I wasn't able to buy the things that I would have liked to at the time, *but saving was more important* because of the lessons I was learning from *The Richest Man in Babylon.*

I know that you'd like to earn more money, but until you do, you have to live with the income you have today. That is the reason you are reading this book – to change your circumstances with money. A budget is another component of the plan to buy a million dollars®.

Let's look at an example that will help you better understand a budget. Sports work on the same principles as a budget does. Here we have two teams.

A		B	
Jets	20 points (lose)	Jets	28 points (win)
Rams	21 points (win)	Rams	21 points (lose)
	-1 Jets		+7 Rams

In example A, the Jets have 20 points *(which represent the income)* and the Rams have 21 points *(the expenses). So the Jets lose by one point.* The Jets have a good offense *(good income)* but a bad defense *(they spend too much)!* In example B, the Jets have 28 points *(the income)* and the Rams have 21 points *(the expenses). So the Jets win by seven points.*

In sports, you lose because your team has a bad defense – it doesn't matter if you have a good offense. You *lose because they score more points than you do.* In football, you can score 50 points, but if the other team scores 51 points, *you still lose.*

It works the same way with your money. You win every month if you have a good income and lose if you spend too much. My advice is to keep track of your expenses through a budget. Start today! Again, this tool will help you to *buy a million dollars®,* as you will see later on.

In this example, we know the score by keeping track during the game. With a budget, you keep track of your expenses during the month to see if you win (earn more than you spend) or lose (spend more than you earn).

In the next chapter, you will learn how your money disappears.

6. WHAT MAKES MONEY DISAPPEAR? (TAXES)

How is it that we start to work when we are 21 to 24 years old and when we reach 40, we have little to show for it? Is it that we aren't taught to think about the future? Is it that we think we have plenty of time to make our money grow? Or is it that we do not have a plan for the future of our money? *We put it off until tomorrow... or someday.*

The younger you start, the less money you need to make it grow into a million dollars. But the older you start, the more money you need. We saw this in Chapter Three.

To better understand this section, you need to understand how taxes make it harder for you to buy a million dollars®. The government collects taxes in order to supply us with services and protection. They are a liability for you because taxes take money out of your pocket. And *you are either taking money out of your pocket or putting it in!*

Learn to Pay Less in Taxes

Taxes are the single biggest expense in your household. In the United States, you work the first five months of the year to pay taxes and the rest of the year to pay yourself. Most people pay up to 40 percent on federal, state (California collects 10 %) and local taxes (property and sales tax). Similarly, in Canada, taxes eat up an average of 48 % of people's income. That's right, almost all of your income is subject to taxes and this is why you need to learn how to protect yourself.

Sadly, a lot of people don't realize that taxes are their biggest expense and they don't know how to pay less.

What you pay in taxes does matter to you. If your goal is to buy your million dollars®, then you need to reduce your taxable income (your net income after deductible expenses). Taxable income is the income you show on your annual tax return.

You need to learn to reduce your net income. If you reduce it through deductions (expenses), you'll pay less in taxes. Paying less in taxes is a way of saving money and the more money you save, the more you can put toward buying a million dollars®.

Let me give you an example of what happens with most people and their taxes. Let's say that at John's workplace, they withhold $500 per month from his salary for taxes. That's about $6,000 per year, right?

At the end of the year, John's accountant calculates his taxes and tells him he will get only $1,000 back from the IRS. John is probably not happy, so he asks his accountant, "Why so little?" The accountant explains that John needs more deductible expenses, but doesn't tell him what other expenses he can use. John knows that what he pays in rent, car and telephone are expenses, but they are personal expenses and he can't declare them on his tax return.

In this way, John sent the IRS or CCRA $6,000 that year and they sent back $1,000 of his own money, without paying him any interest on it. John paid $5,000 that year in taxes because he couldn't find more expenses he could declare.

If John had more deductible expenses to declare on his tax returns, and if those expenses helped him get back an extra $2,000 each year, that would be an extra $2,000 for John.

And if John invests that $2,000 at 10 percent for 20 years, he will have $114,550.00.

I want to show you an example of how your regular

everyday expenses can help you *save on taxes*. In the example, you will see John pay less in taxes when he *declares more expenses*.

How You Pay Taxes

Tax deductions are the "expenses" that you are allowed to subtract from your income. The less income you show after

	Example A	Example B
John earns	$50,000	$50,000
Expenses	$20,000	-$38,000
He then pays taxes on	$30,000	$12,000

taking these deductions, the less you pay in taxes.

As you can see in example A, John must pay taxes on $30,000. In example B, he pays taxes on $12,000. It is the *expenses* he declares that make the difference.

John will pay less in taxes with example B, because he has *$38,000 in deductible expenses*. In example A, John only has *$20,000 in expenses* and that is the key! *The more expenses, the less tax you pay!*

Does the same accountant do your taxes every year? If he isn't helping you to reduce your tax liability, *it's time to change your accountant.* I have changed accountants several times.

But you personally need to learn how to turn many everyday personal expenses into tax-deductible expenses. Tax planning will help you understand and take advantage of the tax code to lower your taxes in ways that are completely legal. Again, when you pay less in taxes, it is *a savings to you, so you can invest more money.*

How Do I Pay Less in Taxes?

You can pay less tax by turning your personal expenses

into business expenses.

If you have a job, you have to file your annual tax return using a "Schedule A." When you have a business, you use an additional set of forms called a "Schedule C." *Schedule C is the secret to paying less in taxes,* because that is where most of the deductions (expenses) are allowed.

The *key is to file both a Schedule A and a Schedule C on your tax return.* How can you do this? By having a home-based business, because the best tax reduction strategy in North America today is a home-based business. In the U.S. and Canada, fiscal law benefits the small business begun from home.

In Canada, you use the T1 tax return, most often the T1 General tax return, to declare the T4 Statements of Remuneration Paid you receive from your employer. However self-employed business people complete the Form T2124 Statement of Business Revenue and Expenses (which is also a part of the T1 General tax return). If you have a job *and* a home business, then you include both the T4 Statement of Employment Information and Form T2124 in your return. Form T2124 is where you can list your deductable expenses.

The government gives you incentives to start a small business, because this is how a lot of the corporations in North America started, like Microsoft Corp., Mrs. Fields Famous Brands LLC, and Apple Computer Inc. They started small and, as they grew, they began to employ more people. The creation of new jobs benefits the economy, so the government offers tax benefits to small home-based businesses to help them grow.

That's what happened to me. I started a small home-based business with Herbalife International and through their Success Training System, it grew steadily. Today, more than 5,000 people work with me in my business, which is run from my home office. This allowed me to turn many of my personal expenses into business expenses and reduce my tax liability. *I took advantage of being self-employed and the tax savings were immediate.*

When you only take the standard deductions (Schedule A) on your tax returns, you pay more taxes. When you itemize deductions (Schedule C), you reduce your tax liability. So the key is to file a Schedule C on your tax return and the only way you can do that is to start a home-based business.

Has your accountant ever explained this to you? I had some accountants who never told me how to pay less in taxes. When I started my Herbalife business, I had to learn what I am sharing with you here.

In the following example, you'll see why you will *pay less in taxes legally.* If you have a business, you can con-

	Employee	Business
Earns	$25,000	$25,000
Deductible Expenses	0	$20,000
Difference	$25,000	$5,000
Taxes	-$5,000	$750
Govenment Returns	$1,000	
Total Taxes Paid	$4,000	$750

vert many of your day-to-day expenses into tax deductions.

Employee vs. Home-Based Business

The employee pays taxes on the $25,000 he earns a year, which is $5,000. He files his tax return and gets back $1,000, without interest, from the IRS or RRSP. The government kept $4,000 and that is what the employee paid in taxes. He doesn't get more money back because he didn't have more deductible expenses.

The business owner pays taxes on the $5,000 he earns *after expenses* (deductions). The key for him was the $20,000 in deductible expenses; obviously he will pay less in taxes. Let's say that his tax rate was 15 percent on the $5,000. He would pay $750 in taxes instead of the $4,000 the employee paid.

What can you do to reduce your tax liability? *Start a home-based business on a part-time basis.*

Why a Home-Based Business?

First of all, with a business of your own that you operate from home, you'll have an additional source of income each month to pay off debt or to save and invest. And at the same time, you will be able to lower your taxes. Remember, the primary objective of starting a business is to generate more income and not to lose money. But a home-based business will bring benefits by permitting you to itemize your deductions, and this will help reduce the amount you pay in taxes.

The key is turning your personal expenses into business expenses.

There are expenses that you have every month that you can't declare in your tax return. But you have to spend that money anyway. Some of these are rent, car costs, car insurance, telephone, utilities, health insurance, Internet fees, computer-related expenses and vacations.

When you have a home-based business, these are some of the services you can use in your part-time business. For example, by having a business, you need an office in your home. You then designate a room for office use only. Then you can deduct the area of that room in square feet as an expense. It works this way.

If you rent an apartment of 1,200 sq. ft. and the room for the office is 400 sq. ft., that room constitutes one-third of the apartment's total area. You are then allowed to declare one-third of the rent as "business office rent." If your rent is $1,200 each month, then one-third, or $400, would be for office rental expense and that's how much you can declare in you tax return. Your accountant will be able to help you with this, so be aware that this strategy is available to you.

You can do the same with other personal expenses you already pay for that can help you with your business.

Let me show you how it works. Let's say that your ex-

Personal Expenses	Bills per Month	Percent You Can Deduct	Current Business Expenses
Rent/house	$900	30%	$270
Utilities	$100	30%	$ 30
Telephone	$100	90%	$ 90
Cell Phone	$ 50	100%	$ 50
Car Payment	$300	80%	$240
Car Insurance	$100	80%	$ 80
Gasoline	$150	80%	$120
Health Insurance	$200	100%	$200
Vacations	$200	100%	$200
Total	$2100		$1,280

penses are like the ones in the following example:

$1,280 x 12 months = $15,360 in expenses per year that you did not have before you started a home-based business.

In the example above, $2,100 are personal expenses you pay for every month, but you cannot use these as deductions (expenses) in your current tax return.

If you have a home-based business, $1,280 per month of personal expenses are turned into business expenses. This is how much you declare in your tax return and how you increase your deductible expenses.

That would be *$15,360 per year that you can use in deductions (expenses).* As a result, you reduce your net income and pay less in taxes, as shown in the following example:

	Employee	Business	
Earns	$25,000	$25,000	Earns
First Pay Taxes	$5,000	$15,360	Deductible Expenses
Get Check	$20,000	$9,640	Difference
Taxable Income	$20,000	$9,640	Taxable Income

You pay taxes on $9,640, instead of paying taxes on $25,000.

The employee first pays his taxes (withheld every pay-day), for a total of $5,000 a year, and might or might not get money back from the government. If he does receive a re-fund, he will not be paid interest on the money the IRS or CCRA held for a whole year. The employee loaned the gov-ernment his money without charging interest… not a bad deal for the government.

The difference with the business owner is that he spent $15,360 first, reducing his net income to $9,640 and paying taxes on this amount at the end of the year.

The employee paid taxes on $25,000 dollars, has very few expenses (Schedule A) and *pays more in taxes*. The business owner paid taxes on a net income of $9,640 dol-lars; he has more expenses and *pays less in taxes*.

Sandra, a friend of mine, has the problem that I just ex-plained. She pays too much in taxes every year. She is a single mother studying for her MBA degree and works full time with a big corporation that pays her very well.

The problem is that she makes a good salary, but cannot buy a house because of the taxes she pays.

One day while talking with her about finances, I couldn't believe it when she told me what she was paying in taxes. It was more than $45,000 a year.

Her accountant wasn't helping her, so she decided to do her own taxes. By filing them herself, she stopped paying additional taxes with her yearly return, but still wasn't able to reduce the amount of taxes that she was paying.

I was amazed to learn that in her MBA program she wasn't learning how to reduce her tax burden, so I met with her to show her how a home-based business could help.

I showed her how she could turn her personal expenses into business expenses by having her own business. She couldn't believe what she learned. She was thrilled to find out she could save $20,000 to $30,000 a year in taxes if she had a home-based business.

What do you think she did? She started a business, be-cause finally someone showed her how she could get the money for the down payment to buy her first house.

You should consider starting a home-based business, because, in addition to the extra income it generates, *the average tax savings for people with a home-based business is from $2,500 to $8,000 per year*. Savings like this can be accomplished very easily once you learn how, and I just showed you the basics to get started.

If you save on your taxes, you'll have more money to buy a million dollars®. *Stop working for the government and start working for yourself!* I'm very glad I did.

Reasons for a home-based business:

1. Start a home-based business. (I started a business with Herbalife.)
2. Have a home office and understand the deductions allowed for home-based businesses.
3. Study the examples I showed you above and ask your accountant how you can implement them.
4. If your accountant doesn't teach you the steps to capitalize on the deductions of a home-based business, look for an accountant who knows about it.
5. Keep a daily diary of receipts from everything you do.
6. Finally, *learn what personal expenses can be used for your home office and turn them into business expenses.*

It doesn't matter where in the English-speaking world you live, because taxes work in pretty much the same way everywhere. A home-based business will not only bring in an additional income, it will also help you pay less in taxes.

Inflation

Income tax is one of the two main reasons your money disappears. The other is inflation. It's important to understand how inflation affects your purchasing power and how it can make you rich or poor.

The things that you purchase today *will be worth more or less in the future* because of inflation! Again, ask yourself the following question, *"Is my money growing in value or is it disappearing in value?"* Make sure you are buying more things that increase in value. That is another key to buying a million dollars®.

Appreciation vs. Depreciation

Let's say you purchase two cars, one used and one new. After a year, the used car goes down (depreciates) less in price than the new one does.

The *used car* and its value after a year of ownership			
Year	Cost	After depreciation	
2002	$25,000	2004	$22,500

The *new car* and its value after a year of ownership			
Year	Cost	After depreciation	
2002	$30,000	2004	$22,500

Here's an example:

You buy both cars at the same time, but the used car goes down in value more slowly because it has a lower depreciation rate. The new car goes down (depreciates) in value by 25 percent as soon as you take it out of the dealership.

Year purchased	Year sold
November, 1999	March, 2002
Price $225,000 ➡	**Price** $335,000

The advice is to *buy a one- or two-year-old used car,* because you lose less money on it.

Now, when you buy a house, it usually goes up in value. Here's an example with the townhouse I purchased in Playa del Rey, California:

If you want to make your money grow, which would

you buy – a car or a house? Of course you'd buy the house. As I mentioned before, you probably don't buy a house because you don't have the down payment, but you need to buy one because inflation will make its value go up in the future.

I have learned to buy one- or two-year-old cars because I know how much money I lose on a new car. I like new cars just like you do, but my priority is to pay as much as possible every month to my savings account.

Again, the reason is because I am counting on turning 60 years old and want to have as much money saved as possible when I get there. I've met a lot of people in my business who are over 55 years old and don't have any savings. I imagine that must be a scary feeling. The more money you have at 60 years old, the better off you will be emotionally.

Other Things that Make Your Money Disappear

As you see, when you buy a car, it makes your money disappear. Besides inflation, here are other things that go down in value:

Television	Clothes	Toys
Computer	Vacations	Utilities
Stereo	Telephones	Taxes
Car	Restaurants	Movies

I'm not saying you shouldn't buy these things. What I am saying is that you need to understand that this is the reason your money doesn't grow. What I recommend to people is to *concentrate on buying things that go up in value.*

Not all used things go down in value – some do go up in value, like antiques.

Understanding inflation is very important in helping you buy a million dollars®. Knowing what makes your money disappear will actually help you make better choices

7. THINGS THAT MAKE YOUR MONEY GROW

Now that you have an idea of how your money disappears, let's talk about the things that make your money grow. If you don't know how money grows, then how are you going to have more of it in the future?

Most of your life you've been earning money and spending it. Even so, you have little to show for it – the money has disappeared.

But you can start to make your money grow by investing it. In the English-speaking world, investments work in basically the same way. If you are fortunate enough to have a parent, a grandparent or a friend who knows how to invest, then you're lucky. You have someone to teach you.

Places to Make your Money Grow

Most people only know about investing with savings accounts and CDs (Certificates of Deposit), both usually opened at a bank. They are almost never told of other options and never learn about other ways to invest. Why do you think that is? We all want to have a lot of money, but we are never shown how to make or accumulate it.

Savings Accounts
The first step is to learn the areas where your money can grow. You know now that you must pay yourself the first 10 percent of everything you earn. You would first invest this

money in a savings account at your bank.

This should be a temporary place to save your money until you have at least $2,000, so you are able to invest it in other places that pay more interest. Savings accounts at banks usually pay you the lowest interest. As I am writing this, they are paying less than 1 percent.

Certificates of Deposit (CD)

Certificates of Deposit are other savings instruments offered by banks. When you invest in a CD, you usually have to commit your money for a period of at least six months. There are also long-term CDs, of one year or more. They will pay you more interest than savings accounts, but you have to keep your money invested for longer periods of time. I have never invested in this manner.

Money Market Funds

Apart from savings accounts and CDs, banks offer other types of accounts for you to invest money. These are called Money Market Accounts, which are not to be confused with Money Market Funds. I have not invested in these.

I personally invest part of my money in *Money Market Funds* at brokerage houses. I call them investment stores and I prefer them because I can get better interest than from banks, no matter how interest rates are doing. I also like them because they are liquid and you are not penalized if you take your money out.

In their investment portfolios, Triana and Kostas have part of their money in these types of accounts. They receive a monthly statement and are able to see how their money is growing.

Bonds

Bonds are another way of investing money. Everything that I have read advises having part of your money invested in these. Bonds consist of money that you lend to a borrower with interest; some of these borrowers are the U.S. government, states, municipalities and corporations.

I personally invest in *Government National Mortgage Association (GNMA) bond funds*. These funds are mortgage-backed bonds and, as I said before, they offer higher interest rates (yields) than savings accounts.

Stocks

When Triana was ten and Kostas eight, I gave them each an imaginary $1,000 to start learning to invest in stocks. I showed them the stock tables in the newspaper and what stocks to look for. Together, we made a list of ten stocks; and from that list, Triana selected a company called World Acceptance Corporation – a company that lends money. The price was $15.90 and she bought 62 shares.

Kostas selected a company called eBay Inc., because he was familiar with it and had used the website to shop. The price of each share of eBay was $103.50 and he bought only nine shares.

After about four weeks, Triana's shares dropped to about $13. She didn't understand why they went down, but I told her that we had done our homework and the price would go back up. And it did. It took another six weeks or so, but the stock increased to more than $20. At that point, we sold it to buy stock in another company.

In two and a half months, Triana made a profit of 24.87 percent. Although she didn't understand how it happened, she learned that stock prices can go up and down. If they go up, she makes money. In this case, she made $245.20 and was so excited that she wanted to learn more about stocks.

With the stock that Kostas bought, there was a different result. eBay went from $103.50 to $116 in price in 15 days and then the stock split in two. When a stock splits, they give you two stocks for each one that you own and then cut the price in half.

His nine shares became 18 shares and the price was around $58 dollars. As I am writing this, it is approximately $63. Kostas has decided to keep them longer and at the moment his profit is some $202.80, or 21.77 percent, in about two and a half months.

That's not bad for their first experience with stocks. The key is not that they understand everything now, but that with time they will understand more about stocks and how they work.

Stocks have an important place in making your money grow, but it takes time to learn by yourself or with the help of a stockbroker. The dilemma is which stocks to buy to make you the most money.

My advice is not to start investing in individual stocks until you understand them. The best way to invest in stocks, if you are just getting started, is through stock mutual funds. I basically invest in these, but today I also invest in stocks, because I understand how they work and like investing in them.

I learned to buy stocks through books and from my stock-brokers. Today I invest in stocks myself, rather than through a broker, because I have done better investing on my own. However, if you are just starting to invest or until you feel you understand stocks, *stick to investing in stock mutual funds, as it is easier and not as risky!*

Mutual Funds

Mutual funds are not hard to understand. I'll try to explain them as I understand them and the way I have used them to make my money grow. Mutual funds use your money and that of other investors to invest in many different companies using money managers.

The money is invested in many ways. You can find mutual funds that are conservative, aggressive and even international in their investing. It's up to you to find out more about each fund, and the best place to do this is at www.morningstar.com. On this website, you can find all the information you need about the mutual fund you are considering. You'll find what the fund invests in, if there are any commissions to pay, the yield, how $10,000 has grown, and the names of the companies where they invest, etc. The website will give you more details.

Once you select a mutual fund, call their toll-free telephone number and ask for a prospectus. Every fund has a minimum dollar amount to begin investing; some start with $500, others start as high as $25,000. The average is around $2,500, but with most funds you can start to invest with between $1,000 and $2,500 dollars.

When you invest your money, you pay a certain price and receive the shares that you bought with the amount you invested. Here's an example:

Amount Invested	Price/Share	Shares
$1,000	$10	100

As you see, you paid $10 per share and own 100 shares. The price of the shares can go up and it can go down. If it goes down, you don't lose money unless you sell your shares. *You only lose money if you sell your shares when the price is down, below what you paid for them.*

The value of your investment will go up or down, and this is why you invest in mutual funds for a long time – five years or more. The following table shows an example of how a stock goes down, but then comes back up.

Amount Invested	Price/Share	Shares
$1,000	$10.00	100
$ 950	9.50	100
$ 900	9.00	100
$ 925	9.25	100
$ 975	9.75	100
$1,025	10.25	100
$1,050	10.50	100
$1,100	11.00	100

Mutual funds work in a very simple way. The question

is, which do I select? I have invested in different mutual funds and I found them by reading financial magazines and by doing my homework through www.morningstar.com.

Let me review a few things you should know about mutual funds. Then I'll tell you which funds I have been investing in and this can give you an idea of where to start.

Things to Know

1. Mutual funds are the best way to start investing in the stock market.
2. The stocks have grown around 11.6 percent per year in the U.S.
3. They are professionally managed.
4. Invest for the long run.
5. They are part of the plan to buy a million dollars®.
6. Invest in no-load mutual funds (no commissions to buy or sell).
7. Invest in one with a yearly fee of less than 1.0 percent. The lower the number, the better, because it means less cost per year and your money grows faster.
8. Start with index funds.

Index Funds

The mutual funds I personally like and invest in are index funds. Index funds invest on the different stock market indexes, like the NASDAQ, the S&P 500 Index and many more. The 500 Index Fund invests in the 500 biggest corporations in America and the Total Stock Market Index invests in the 5,000 biggest corporations in America.

The reason I like these funds is because over long periods of time – like ten to 20 years – it's hard to beat their yield and, if you are just beginning, *this is the best way to get started investing in the stock market.*

Of everything that I have read on mutual funds, index funds had the most favorable reasons to start investing in them. After learning and understanding their benefits, I now invest exclusively in index funds for my retirement account. The reasons are:

1. They have grown over 10 percent each year over a long time.
2. There are no commissions and very low annual fees, less than 0.50 percent.
3. Your money grows more because of the low yearly fees.
4. Very few funds can beat their performance.
5. If you are just getting started, this is the best way to start.
6. If you know how they work, they can make you a millionaire.

If I were 20 years old again, I would start to invest in index funds. I would invest either with *the 500 Index Fund or the Total Stock Market Index Fund.* As I said, this is where I personally have my retirement money invested and I use Vanguard Mutual Funds, because their fees are the lowest of all index funds in the industry.

If three companies have 500 Index Funds and their yearly fees are 0.48 percent, 0.45 percent, 0.40 and 0.18 percent, in which one would you invest? Of course – the one with 0.18 percent fee, and that's why I use The Vanguard Company.

I'm sharing my own mutual funds preferences and why I've chosen them. They are not the only options and you'll want to investigate others, always comparing the annual fees they charge.

In the second part of this book, you'll see how index funds are part of how I am buying a million dollars®.

Real Estate

Real estate is one of the best ways to make your money grow, because the price of a house will keep track with inflation and will go up in price. A house will cost more in the future than it does now. The longer it takes you to buy a house, the more you'll pay, so I believe the sooner you buy a house, the better.

In September of 1999, my landlord asked if I wanted to purchase the townhouse I was renting from her. I knew it was a great house in a great neighborhood and because I had owned real estate before, I wasn't afraid to invest in it. So I said yes.

We agreed on a price of $225,000. We were both happy and closed escrow in November of 1999. About nine months later, a townhouse across from mine sold for about $270,000 and I was very excited. At the same time, I was looking to purchase a house because, although the townhouse was great, it was getting small for Triana, Kostas and me.

On December 21, 2001, I made an offer on a house in Playa del Rey, California, with a great view of the Santa Monica Bay. On December 27, my offer was accepted and escrow closed in March of 2002.

I then decided to sell the townhouse I had purchased in 1999, and put it on the market. The California real estate market was very hot and everything was selling fast. To my surprise, the first day the townhouse was on the market I received eight offers. I couldn't believe it!

I accepted an offer of $335,000, giving me a profit of $110,000 in a year and a half. As I am writing this book, the house that I purchased and am currently living in, is worth more than $1,000,000.

The sooner you buy a house, the better, because its value will go up in the future. So start investing in real estate as soon as possible.

A Business

A business is a great way of making your money grow, and I know from personal experience. I started my Herbalife business in December of 1980 with $29.95 and a $500 investment for an inventory of products. It took me two months to get my investment back, and by using my profits to expand the business, I have made it grow in ten countries.

Today my business has sales of about $12,000,000 per year and I do everything out of my home-based office. That's not bad for a minimum dollar investment.

A business is great, but a home-based business is an even better way to get started for the average person. With a home-based business:

1. You can start with a small investment.
2. You can work out of your home.
3. There's no commute.
4. You have no boss
5. You set the schedule.
6. You can be near your kids while you work.
7. There's no limit to your income.
8. You can save from $2,000 to $10,000 in taxes.
9. The owner of a business earns more than the employees.

If you want to make your money grow, a home-based business is a better option than a job. It should be part of your plan to buy a million dollars®.

I just explained the best ways I know to make your money grow. It doesn't matter where you are, because in the English-speaking world, taxes and investements basically work in the same way. You don't have to fully understand them, just be aware of how they work. In the second part of the book, I will explain how to use them to make your money grow into a million dollars.

8. THE EIGHTH WONDER OF THE WORLD

Albert Einstein said that compound interest "is the greatest mathematical discovery of all time" and "is the eighth wonder of the world."

I remember that in high school they talked to us about *compound interest,* but I didn't understand it, just like I didn't understand a lot about math. In school, they never taught me how *compound interest* would help me become a millionaire, and they didn't give me any examples. We still aren't taught how it can affect our finances, either in a positive way (making your money grow) through investments or in a negative way (making your money disappear) with credit cards.

Math wasn't my favorite subject. I didn't like it and had a hard time passing the tests. Now that I'm older, I've learned that math is very important in all our lives, especially when dealing with our money. I understand how compound interest has a tremendous impact on our finances, and I try to teach everyone how to apply it to his or her own personal economy.

You don't have to be a math whiz. All you have to understand is that compound interest is one of several simple concepts that will make your money grow. Perhaps you think it works too slowly and you need faster solutions to your money problems. But understanding these concepts will help you have the necessary patience to see your money grow and make you a millionaire.

Compound interest is interest earned on both the principal and the interest earned every month. It permits us to bring in interest on the principal (money invested) and also on the interest as it accumulates. If you have $1,000 at 10 percent interest, at the end of one year you have $100 earned in interest.

Then you add it to the $1,000, so that in the second year you start with $1,100. And at the end of that second year, you have $110 in interest.

Compound Interest		
1st year	$1,000 at 10% =	$100 in interest
2nd year	$1,100 at 10% =	$110 in interest
3rd year	$1,210 at 10% =	$121 in interest

If you continue to do this at 10 percent, you'll notice that the money will double in 7.2 years. This is the secret of *compounding interest* – it *will double your money!* The time it takes to do so will vary, according to the interest rate you get. The higher the interest rate, the faster your money will double.

Time it Takes to Double Your Money at:	
5% you can double your money in	14.2 years
8% you can double your money in	9.0 years
10% you can double your money in	7.2 years
15% you can double your money in	4.8 years
20% you can double your money in	3.6 years

It is very important to understand the table above, so you realize how *compound interest* can either get you into debt or help you become a millionaire.

If you owe money, your debt will double against you.

If you have investments, they will double in your favor.

Silvia and Compound Interest

I recently went to Guadalajara, Mexico to teach a class on how to make your money grow, and in the audience was the daughter of a friend of mine. Her name is Silvia and she is only 11 years old. Silvia had taken my class four times before, but had a hard time understanding what compound interest is.

This last time was no exception and, during one of the breaks, she told me again that she didn't understand how compound interest works. She asked me if it was really important to understand it. I told her that it was, because *compound interest can make you rich or make you poor.* I asked her if she wanted to have a lot of money when she grew up, and she said, "Yes!" So I told her she needs to understand how it can help her make her money grow.

The course lasted from 5 p.m. to 9 p.m. At around 7 p.m., her mother said she needed to go home to do homework because it was a school night. But Silvia wanted to hear the rest of my talk, so that she could finally understand compound interest. Her mother told her that if she went home, she could come in the morning instead of going to school, and that made her happy. Silvia returned the following day to listen to the class again and, by the end of it, she finally understood compound interest. Can you imagine the education this 11-year-old got by attending this type of class?

I know Silvia and this is what surprises me about her – she likes to listen and learn about money, she takes notes and applies what she learns. She learned to open a savings account and understands why it is important to have one. She has more than $300 saved in a money market fund to which she continues to add money. Another reason Silvia wants to save is because she knows that Triana and Kostas do.

Again, what are you teaching your children about money?

Time, Consistency and Patience

One of the most important things you should understand about compound interest is that it works over a long period of time, it does so consistently, and you have to be patient.

Since I haven't won the lottery and I don't know if I will, I've had to rely on compound interest to make me a millionaire. Once I understood that over time it would make my money grow into double what I had, that's where I concentrated my investing. *An investor is helped by time,* so the sooner you start to save and invest, the better off you'll be.

Patience has helped me to make better investment decisions and not be afraid to invest. If you have patience, then you can have the things you want in life in the future. And *the future is what counts in making your money grow.*

It is very important to be consistent with everything we do in life. I learned this when I played sports in high school. I also learned that I had to be consistent with my children. The younger my children were, the more consistent I had to be with them. If you are not consistent with your children when they are between the ages of one month and nine years old, the more difficult they will be when they are teenagers. In the same way, we need to be consistent with our savings, so as not to have problems in the future.

In Chapter Two, I explained how interest can work against you or in your favor. Don't let compound interest work against you. *Negative compound interest shrinks wealth. Positive compound interest builds wealth.* It's important to understand the difference.

Remember, negative compound interest is the interest you pay on money you borrow, like credit cards and auto loans. Positive compound interest is the interest that you are paid for your investments, like savings accounts, income funds and the growth of stocks.

Now let's get to the details on how to use compound interest to make your money grow.

Double Your Money

Let's say that your money doubles every five years and, for the next example, let's not consider any interest rate. What would happen to your money with compound interest? Let's take a look.

Every 5 Years Your Money Doubles	
Year 1	$10,000
Year 5	$20,000
Year 10	$40,000
Year 15	$80,000
Year 20	$160,000
Year 25	$320,000
Year 30	$640,000
Year 35	$1,280,000

Notice how the $10,000 doubles. But when does it increase the most? In the first five years, or between year 30 and year 35?

As you can see, it increases more when it doubles between year 30 and 35. Why? It doubles because of compound interest, and it increases more in the future because you have more money during the last five years than you had in the first five.

It is very important for you to understand this example, so that you can be patient with your investments and learn that everything in investing happens in the future. If you make the wrong decisions, there will be no money in the future.

In the next example, let's suppose that my two children start to save money and invest it. Kostas starts when he is 19 years old and *saves and invests for seven years,* but Triana starts to save and invest at the age of 26 *for 25 years.* Take a look at what happens.

	Kostas	Triana
Saves per month	$166.66	$166.66
Saves per year	$2000	$2000
For	7 years	25 years
Annual Interest	10%	10%
Amount Invested	$14,000	$50,000

	Kostas		Triana	
Age	Yearly Investment	Total w/ Interest	Yearly Investment	Total w/ Interest
19	$2000			
20	$2000			
21	$2,000			
22	$2,000			
23	$2,000			
24	$2,000			
25	$2,000	$19,415		
26		$22,106	$2,000	$ 2,084
30		$58,953	$2,000	$12,575
35		$93,648	$2,000	$32,279
40		$148,760	$2,000	$63,153
45		$236,305	$2,000	$111,530
50		$411,774	$2,000	$187,332

Kostas only saves and invests *$2,000 each year for seven years*, for a total of $14,000. Triana saves *$2,000 each year for 25 years, for a total of $50,000.* Why does Kostas have $411,774 at the age of 50 and Triana only has $187,332 at the age of 50?

The answer is compound interest. The sooner you invest, the more help compound interest will give you because it has more time to work. Remember, compound interest is helped by time, and all you need is patience.

When Triana started saving the $2,000 a month, Kostas already had saved $19,415 (with interest) and that made all the difference; Kostas started earlier. The key with saving and investing is *the sooner, the better.*

The Lesson of Time

I recommend that you begin showing your children the examples in this book as soon as possible. Start teaching them about a saving and investing plan and explain why it is important to *start investing at an early age.*

When I saw the previous example, it made all the difference in my approach to investing. What I concentrated on doing was just saving and investing every month. If I missed a month, I treated it like not paying myself, like I'd missed paying the phone bill.

Time goes by really quickly and we're not often aware of it. We don't notice what happens with our money because we always have money problems. When we concentrate on these problems, instead of on saving and investing for the future, we end up not having any money saved.

It is important for me to teach Triana and Kostas about time and investing and how compound interest works, because I was never taught this. Now that I understand these concepts, I need to teach them to my children so they learn to handle money in a positive way. I showed them the following example to give them a better idea of how much money they will have by the time they are 20 years old.

Your Age	If You Save per Month	When You Are	Money You'll Have
10 years	$ 0	20 years	$ 0
10 years	$100	20 years	$20,484
15 years	$100	20 years	$ 7,744
10 years	$ 0	20 years	$ 0
10 years	$200	20 years	$40,969
15 years	$200	20 years	$15,487

With this example, Triana and Kostas were able to understand that if they don't save, they won't have any money by the time they are 20 years old. They also learned that it's better to save $200 a month than $100 a month, because that way they will end up with more.

I personally understand better when I see examples like the one above because I am a visual person. That's why I teach my children with this type of example.

Use Calculators

I started using the Internet to learn more about investing, because there are a lot of tools online that can help you plan for your financial future.

I recommend that you go to www.money.com and www.yahoo.com and visit their saving and retirement calculators to experiment with making plans for your money. *After this exercise, you'll have a different view about what you are doing with your money and can start to make changes.*

First, I use these calculators to help me plan my future and to see how my money is growing. Also, I want to see how much it will grow by the time I'm 60 years old. Seeing these calculations on the Internet gives me an idea of whether I'm on track with my plans.

In addition, I use these calculators to teach my children about money, how it grows, and how much they will have when they are older. They get a better idea because they are learning about math in school. Using the calculators makes it fun for them to see how mathematical principles work to make their money grow.

When Kostas used the Internet calculators, he wanted to know how much a "trillion billion" is. He's fascinated by big numbers and of course he asks me *"Papa, if I had a trillion billion dollars, what could we do?"* And my answer – as usual– is, "Go around the world in 80 days."

One of the things I did with the Internet calculators was

to figure out the different ways that my money would become a million dollars with different interest rates. I suggest that you do the same. Once you see it in print, your imagination will do the rest.

The calculators are derived from math formulas that are based on compound interest and they have been calculated for you. Learn to use them. Like anything else, it just takes practice.

Different mutual fund companies have calculators on their websites to help you prepare for retirement. They will help you with a plan, and then all you do is save and invest your money with them.

9. THE PLAN TO BUY A MILLION DOLLARS®

We don't plan to get into debt; we usually never even think about it. We get into debt quietly, without notice and by ignoring the signs along the way, *because of lack of planning.* Sadly, people who get into debt become poor.

It happens through personal neglect, excess spending, not saving and not planning. If you don't understand how you can get into debt and become poor, then you won't understand how to become rich.

To buy a million dollars® *you must have a plan and work the plan.*

Have a Plan

Do you build a house with plans or without them?

Most people don't accomplish their dreams for lack of planning, wanting everything today and not thinking about the future.

The future is what counts. I've told you that one of my goals is to have good health and money by the time I'm 60. Why 60 years old?

In North America, we think of retiring from our jobs around the age of 60. For us, this decade is one of golden years when we can enjoy our favorite hobbies and pursue our dreams.

The question is, will we accomplish this? With a plan, yes! I don't want to reach 60 and still have to work. *I want to have the option to work if I want to.* How many people do you know who are still working at 60 years of age because *they have to, not because they want to?*

If you know people who are 60 years old and still working, *ask them why they still work.* Ask your parents, your family and your friends' parents if they had plans for their money when they where younger. Did they save and invest consistently for their retirement? Ask them what they would have done differently with their money if they were young again.

I always ask people this question – do you have a plan to buy a million dollars®? What are you doing every single day to be financially independent when you are 60 years old?

To build a house, you need a dream of the house you would like to have and an architect will put that dream on paper. He will draw the plans for the house that you want, but you cannot build the house without plans.

Whether you want to do good things or bad things, you need a plan.

I recently saw the movie *The Italian Job* about how a group of men plan to steal 35 million dollars in gold bars in Venice, Italy. The heist had to be very well planned because of the short period of time they had to carry it out. Of course, they were able to rob the gold in a very precise manner and within the brief timeframe they had. It was very exciting to watch their plan in action.

For these men to be able to steal the gold, they had to plan it very well because their future depended on it.

When you go to the airport and get on a plane, the captain has a flight plan, which he explains as you take off. Can you imagine what could happen if he didn't have a flight plan?

Have you ever thought of starting a business? If you did, you'd need a business plan that would tell you what to do for the business to be successful. Would you plan to sell it in a month or two, or would you plan to keep the business for a long time? This would depend on the plan.

Do you have a plan for the future of your money? How much time do you spend working on it?

I will lay out a simple plan for you that has worked for me. You're going to need to keep an eye on your plan and review it once or twice a month, just as you keep an eye on your children as they grow up. *If you take care of your money, it will grow well, just like your children.*

The plan is simple. If you don't understand part of it, you can ask someone or just go to our website www.buyamilliondollars.com and ask.

The ideas and advice I give you are easy to understand. If I could grasp them, I'm sure you can too. They worked for me. I made a lot of mistakes that have cost me time and money, but I learned from my mistakes and – *more important – I didn't give up!*

The goal of this plan is to make your money grow 10 to 15 percent per year over a long period of time. When I say over a long period of time, I mean 10, 20 or 30 years in the future – it all depends on how old you are and when you start.

As write this, I am looking at an ad that says, "get your share of today's 300%-1,300% growth stock moves," "turn $69 into millions." I am always getting emails promising that you can earn 50 percent through their system. I also get emails claiming that you can make $10,000 in three months.

Can this really be true? It might be, with a plan.

Sergio is a cousin of mine who lives in Mexico. He has a good job and is earning a good salary by Mexico's standards, but he wasn't going anywhere financially. He had been trying to make big money through investments that he had found on the Internet, some of the same ones I just shared.

In the summer of 2002, he came to me for advice. I started asking him questions and realized that he didn't have a plan and was trying to invest with his emotions. But the most important thing was that he was willing to learn and that he didn't owe any money to anyone.

I gave him a plan to follow. *First, start saving. Second, start investing. Third, look for other avenues to earn income and last, start thinking about buying a house.*

In November of 2003, I had another of many conversations with him and we talked about his progress. He was saving with a plan and a goal. He had found two other ways of making money without quitting his present job, and he had just made the down payment on his first house.

I was excited for him. Now he understands why he and many others do not get ahead financially – they don't have a plan. *Start with a plan and follow it.*

A Plan with Compound Interest

Before I show you the plan, I want to explain how retirement accounts work, because they are an important part of making your money grow.

Your investment plan will need the help of retirement accounts, so that the government will not interfere with the growth of your money through taxes.

Retirement accounts were created for you to make your money grow (invest), without paying taxes on that money until you retire and use it. The government lets you put money into the account year after year, without taxing you on the interest you make. This enables compound interest to do its job and make your money grow faster. In Chapter Four, you learned how taxes can make your money disappear instead of helping it grow.

In the U.S., you can start taking money out of the account when you are 59 ½ years old, and at that time the government will tax you at the current tax rate. You can choose to take it out or continue to let it grow – it's all up to you.

In Canada, you can contribute savings and eligible investments to a registered retirement savings plan (RRSP) for future use. These deposits reduce your taxable income and you can defer taxes up until you turn 70. However, if you withdraw funds before that time, the money will be included in your taxable income for that year. At the age of 70, the RRSP will be closed and you can withdraw the account balance in full and include it in your taxable income. Or you can use the account balance to purchase either an annuity or a registered retirement income fund (RRIP), and specify amounts to be withdrawn each year in the future. These will then be included each year in taxable income.

With retirement accounts, the most important thing is this: *Put money into the account every month.* This is the best way to save money and not pay taxes until you take it out.

We've already seen that you have to pay yourself first (save). You realize that compound interest will make your money grow and make you rich by the time you reach 60 years of age. Now that you understand why your money can best grow in a retirement account, I'd like to talk about four U.S. retirement accounts and two Canadian retirement accounts that affect most people.

IRAs

Individual retirement accounts, or IRAs as they are known, let every individual who works put money into the account tax-free. It is taxed when you can take it out at 59 ½ years of age or later.

First, you open the account at any bank or financial institution. Once it is open, you can deposit up to $4,000 in 2005 (per individual). Check what the amounts will be for 2003.

Second, if you take the money out before you reach 59 ½ years of age, you pay a 10 percent penalty and also pay taxes on the amount you withdraw. A friend of mine took $14,000 out of his account and it cost him $3,000 between the penalty and the income taxes he had to pay – a very expensive lesson. Don't take the money out before you are permitted to.

Third, you can invest this money in saving accounts, CDs, money market accounts, mutual funds, stocks, bonds and real estate, etc.

Roth IRA

The Roth-IRA takes its name from the U.S. senator who introduced it. With the Roth-IRA, you pay taxes on the money you put into the account before you deposit it. When you take out the money after 59 ½ years old, you do not pay taxes. To me, this is a better option than the traditional IRA.

First, open the account at a bank or financial institution. Just as with the IRA, you can deposit $4,000 per individual in 2004.

Second, just like the IRA, if you take the money out before you reach 59 ½ years of age, you pay a 10 percent penalty and also pay taxes. *Again, do not take out your money. It's too expensive.*

Third – just like with the traditional IRA – you can invest the money in savings accounts, money market accounts, CDs, mutual funds, bonds, stock and real estate.

401(K) retirement accounts.

If you work at a company that offers you this account, take advantage of it.

First, open it at the financial institution your company has chosen. Your company will match the money you deposit, for up to 15 percent of your annual earnings, as long as the amount does not exceed the legal cap of $10,000. For example, if the percentage the company chooses is 6 percent, you put 6 percent of your income in and they will add an additional 6 percent. I insist, if they offer it, take advantage of it – they are giving you extra money for working there. Contributions are pre-tax, meaning the employer deducts the amount from your salary *before* calculating income taxes.

Second, they will offer options on where to invest, just

like the IRA or Roth-IRA. You have to ask at your company about your choices, such as CDs, money market accounts, mutual funds, bond funds, etc.

Third, you can't take the money out, but if you change jobs, you can take the account with you. This is called a rollover. You need to follow the rules on how to take it with you. Ask at your new job or ask your accountant.

Self-Employed Individual Retirement Accounts
Known as SEP-IRAs, self-employed individual retirement accounts allow an individual who is self-employed to make deductible contributions to the retirement account. You do not pay taxes on this money until you take it out at retirement.

You can contribute up to 15 percent of your net income or $30,000, whichever is less. If you are *self-employed or have a home-based business, take advantage of this type of account,* because you can save more money this way.

First, you can invest the money just like you do in the other plans. You open an account at a bank or financial institution. They will help you to set it up; you just need to be aware of these different accounts.

Second, you must pay a penalty (in addition to taxes) if you take the money out before retirement age. Again, do not take it out. It's too expensive.

In Canada, there are two options for investing funds for retirement and they work in similar ways.

Registered Retirement Savings Plan (RRSP)
Whether you have a job or a business in Canada, you can deposit up to 18 percent of the previous year's income in a registered retirement savings plan (RRSP). Employers can make RRSP contributions on behalf of their employees, but such amounts would be included in income by the employees for that year.

These accounts are usually – but not always – exclusively for retirement.

The RRSP is closed once you reach the age of 70, and you must choose one of the following options:

1. Withdraw the account balance in full and include this amount or any part of it as income for that year
2. Withdraw the account balance in full and purchase an annuity. You will set the amounts to be withdrawn each year in the future and included as annual income.
3. Withdraw the amount in full and purchase a registered retirement income fund (RRIP) with prescribed minimum amounts withdrawn each year in the future and included in income annually.

The maximum annual contribution for 2005 is $16,500, and the RRSP can defer taxes up to the year you become 70 years old.

Registered Pension Plans (RPP)

Canadian employers may also set up registered pension plans (RRP) for their employees. Both the employers and the employees may make contributions to the RRP within the prescribed combined limits for RRSPs and RPPs, whereby a part of the employee's income may be tax deferred until age 70.

Different Places to Invest

You need to learn where to invest your money (make it grow), because most people only put it in banks. I personally do not invest at banks, because they usually pay less interest and offer fewer investment choices than other financial institutions do.

I have a relationship with one bank where I keep money to be able to write checks and pay bills. The bank that I use doesn't charge me to use their website to pay bills. That's why I use this bank, but I don't invest there.

Brokerage houses – which I call investment stores – like Charles Schwab & Co, Inc., Fidelity Brokerage Services, LLC and The Vanguard Group, Inc. are great places to invest. Become familiar with their services and fees. They offer better options to make your money grow.

Another place to invest your money is in mutual fund companies, like Vanguard, and Dodge and Cox. I personally use Vanguard because their fees are low, but I also use Dodge and Cox for some investments.

I think the best options for investing are brokerage houses and mutual fund companies, because they help you with a plan and you can make your money grow through their investments. Do your homework by visiting their websites to see what they offer and what their fees are.

When you invest, you first want to do it inside your retirement account, until you reach the maximum amount allowed. Then you can do the same thing outside of your retirement account.

The main reason you first invest inside your retirement account is that you keep the government from interfering in making your money grow by taxing it. You also give compound interest the best chance to make you a millionaire. You want to invest your money in your retirement account by implementing the investment plan in the next section.

Of course, there are many plans to invest your money, but the plan in the next chapter is the one that has worked for me. It's a simple one to get started without too much knowledge of investing in the stock market.

The next section explains the plan to buy a million dollars®. Don't worry if you don't understand it in the beginning; that isn't important. *The important thing is that you start.* Remember, when children learn something new, they don't understand it at first, but with practice they begin to. *Don't make it complicated. If it makes sense to you, just do it!*

PART TWO

THE 1/3 – 2/3
INVESTMENT PLAN

10. THE 1/3 OF
YOUR INVESTMENT PLAN

Since I started my business, I've learned that you have ups and downs with money. When things are going well, you don't pay attention to your money, because you think that your financial situation isn't going to change or it will only get better. But you discover that things do change with your job or business and you get into trouble because you don't have money in your savings account. Isn't that what happens to all of us, at one time or another?

When we have money problems, we either go to our parents or to the bank to borrow some money. This can hold us over for a few months until things start to improve. But if we cannot borrow money from these sources, then we have problems with the people to whom we owe money.

At times, I have done extremely well financially. And at other times, things haven't gone well at all. Because of these experiences, I've learned to always keep money in a money market fund for a rainy day.

It is important to me to have this money in case I have an emergency. In baseball, relief pitchers are there to help the starting pitchers when they have problems; relief pitchers help the team to get out of trouble in any given inning. In the same way, my savings help me face unexpected problems.

I have been teaching Triana and Kostas to save for their future because of my experiences in the past. I tell my children that the reason people have problems with money is that they don't save or have money for emergencies. The more I explain, the more they understand, but they will understand it even better someday. I tell them that I explain things is so that it will be easier for them in the future.

A Suggestion

This is what I do and suggest you do too, because you never know when things will change for you financially. I have 1/3 of my money in cash (liquid) as *savings accounts or money market accounts.*

This is the money I put away for a rainy day. If I have this money, I don't worry because I know it will be available in an emergency. Remember, *"there is never a right time to get a flat tire,"* and you never know when you will have an emergency.

Here is my rule for that money for rainy days – *have an emergency money fund equal to what it costs you to live for eight months.* For example, if your total monthly expenses are $3,000, multiply this number by eight. Thus you should have $24,000 in liquid funds (in a savings account or money market account). This way, you know you will be all right for eight months.

This rule has always saved me in emergencies, because I knew that I couldn't go to my parents for a loan when I had a money problem. *Remember, our financial life is full of ups and downs, but what matters is how we plan for those ups and downs.*

Next, Buy a House

You may believe you can't buy a house because you think the price is too high. The real reason you don't buy a house is that *you don't have the down payment.*

You don't have the money for the down payment because you don't save for it.

Save for the Down Payment

Once you've saved enough money for a rainy day, you can continue to save to purchase a house.

If you think about it, *you already are buying a house – not your house, but somebody else's!* If you're renting, then you are paying the mortgage for the person who owns the house or the apartment where you live; you are helping them buy their house.

When you buy a house, you don't pay the full price of the house at once. Instead, you make monthly payments. *If you can afford the monthly payments, then you can afford to buy the house.* Today there are so many different types of loans that there's no excuse not to buy a house. Start saving for the down payment.

Where Do I Get the Money?

Let's say that the city where you live has an average house price of $200,000 and that you need 10 percent for the down payment, or $20,000 dollars, right?

What I would do is divide $20,000 by 24 months. That makes $833.33 that I would have to save each month to come up with the down payment in two years. If this is too much for you, then divide it by 36 months. That is how you come up with the down payment to buy your first house.

Price	$200,000
Down payment 10%	-$ 20,000
Amount of loan	$180,000
Down payment of $20,000 divided by 24 months =	$833.33
Down payment of $20,000 divided by 36 months =	$555.55

You either save $833.33 or $555.55 per month to have the down payment for the house.

Remember, in Chapter Four I explained how you could save more money on your taxes by having a *home-based business.* With a home-based business, you can save $100 to $200 per month in taxes and *make an extra $300 to $500 per month* by promoting your service or product.

I was able to buy my first house in 1983 with the money I made from my Herbalife home-based business. If I had continued to work at a job, I don't think I would have been able to purchase a house in the Los Angeles area because of the prices. I don't know how a newly married couple can buy their first house in California without having a home-based business.

Reasons to Buy a House

There are three reasons you want to buy a house. The first is that it keeps up with inflation and it increases in value over time.

The second is pride of ownership and a better standard of living. This is especially important if you have children. Children do compare where they live to where their friends live. I know this because my own children tell me about their friends' houses and their bedrooms. *Don't kid yourself thinking this makes no difference in your family's life. It does!* If you aren't currently buying a house and are renting, then explain to your children why you don't live in your own home when they ask you about it. And yes, they will ask you.

The third reason is that a house is part of the plan for *buying a million dollars®*. Its value is going up and the amount of money you owe is going down, so by the time you are 60 years old or even sooner, you'll have the million dollars in equity and you will own the house free and clear.

The Most Important Thing

When you are buying a house, make sure that you *pay additional money toward the principal.* This will enable you to pay off the house faster and save a lot on interest. Look at your loan papers and see how much you will pay in interest by the time you finish paying it. Can you believe it?

Save on the interest by prepaying the principal on the loan. Look at the table below to see how much you can save per month in interest if you make additional payments. I'll show you this example in round numbers, because it is easier to understand if, like me, you aren't good at math.

Let's say your monthly mortgage payment is $1,000 per month. The payments are structured something like this:

Payment	Interest Portion	Principal Portion	Amount You Pay
1	$950	$50	$1000
2	$948	$52	$1000
3	$946	$54	$1000

Now, let's look at two examples and say that you make additional payments toward the principal.

You make the first payment of $1,000, plus the portion of the principal for the second month of $52. The following month you pay $1,052 dollars. Your *savings would be $952 on the interest portion!*

Again, you just *saved $948* by paying more toward the principle:

Payment	Principal Portion	Next Payment	You Save in Interest
$1,000	$52	$1,052	$948

Now look at this example. You make the first payment of $1,000, the portion of the principal for the second month of $52 and the portion of the principal for the third month of $54, or $106 extra next month.

The payment would be $1,106 and your savings would be $948 of the *interest portion* of payment number two, plus $946 of the *interest portion* on payment number three. *That's a total savings of $1894 of interest!*

Payment	Principal Portion	Next Payment	You Save in Interest
$1,000	$106	$1,106	$1,894

That's right, when you make additional payments toward the principal, you save money. Again, if you don't totally understand this, ask your lending company to explain it to you. I also recommend that you get a book called *A Banker's Secret* by Marc Eisenson, who does a great job explaining mortgage payments. This book was an eye opener for me. Read it!

This is the first part of *buying a million dollars*® and, as you can see, it isn't as difficult as you thought. You just need to learn and understand a bit more about the different topics I've talked about.

The second part of *buying a million dollars*® is the 2/3 investment plan. I call this plan the million-dollar portfolio, because I thought the only people who had portfolios were millionaires. If you implement it, you too will have a portfolio that will buy your million dollars.

It doesn't matter what country you live in – you'll obtain your million with a plan, with time and with patience, if you are consistent in putting these concepts to work. Again, the key is to start now.

11. THE 2/3 INVESTMENT PLAN (HOW TO BUY A MILLION DOLLARS®)

For a very long time, I looked for the right investment system to make my money grow. Since I didn't know anyone who invested in the stock market, I started to look for ways to learn to invest. I decided that books, magazines and my stockbroker would be my teachers.

I lost money and I made money, but my money didn't seem to grow and I was very confused. At times, I became frustrated and impatient with everything that I was doing, *but I kept looking.* My goal was always to make my money grow until it became a million dollars.

One of my hobbies is going to bookstores to study book titles in the investment and personal finance sections. The ones with the word "million" always catch my eye. Through this, I started to get some idea of what I needed to become a better investor. But everything I tried seemed too complicated for me.

I read and tried out different ideas. Some worked and some didn't, but I started to get better at investing. As things began to work and I started to see my money grow through the monthly statements, I started to believe more in what I was doing. I had more confidence. I kept investing and kept learning from my mistakes. I learned to keep my emotions out of my investment decisions and, little by little, I started to define my investment rules.

I did this by reading more and actually investing. The

more I read, the better I did, the more confidence I had, and the easier it became. Instead of trying to make a lot of money quickly, I realized that I had *a better chance to make my money grow to a million dollars over a long period of time.*

I had to do this consistently every month. I found I needed to keep track of what I was doing. I had to follow through with my plans and I had to be patient. I needed to make sure I saved money every month to invest, in order to make it grow.

I had to remain focused on my investment plan of action. This helped me to take out the emotional part that is attached to your money as you invest it.

When my investments would go down in value, I'd ask myself "Am I doing the right thing?" "Is this stock's price going to go down even more?" "Is this going to work?" To keep myself from doubting my decisions, I'd just review the rules I set for myself and go back to some of the books I had read to reassure myself that I was making the right decisions.

But as things started to work for me, I just kept doing what was working the best. I started to keep notes on my progress, because no one was teaching me. I couldn't ask anyone if I was doing the right thing – I was learning by myself. Finally, everything began to come together to give me more confidence in my investment plan.

Making Your Money Grow
Is Like Raising Your Children

When I found out I was going to have my first child, I decided I wouldn't do certain things that I remember not liking as a child. But I was going to do things that I liked when I was young. I decided to follow certain guidelines when it came to my children, and I knew I had to be consistent with them. I learned by doing, just like many of you. *All I did was pay attention to my children and use common sense; it was easy and practical.*

When I was learning to invest, I applied the same tactics. You will learn in the same way – by asking others, reading, investing and paying attention when you invest.

Taking care of your children when they are young will prepare you for when they are teenagers. Adolescence is the most difficult period you'll have with your children. It's the same way with money. *You want to take care of your money when you are young, because if you don't, you'll have financial problems when you get older.*

Have a Plan

There were seven things I wanted my children to learn, to experience and to do well as they were growing up. Some of these things helped me one way or another in life and some things were very difficult for me, like math. Here they are:

1. Learn to read and write well
2. Be good at math
3. Learn a second language (Spanish)
4. Travel
5. Practice an individual sport
6. Play a team sport
7. Learn about money

I had only seven ideas of what I wanted to teach my children and these were the foundation for their education. Over time, they changed for the better, but these were the first ideas.

I believe the same is true about your finances. You must have ideas of what you want to accomplish with your money over time. You acquire these ideas by reading and experimenting. *We don't think about money until we have money problems, right?*

Do you have a plan for the money you earn? You need to have a plan for your money to grow. Do you have one?

My Plan

This is my own personal plan. I'm sharing it to give you an idea of where to begin.

My intention is to motivate you to learn about mutual funds, and which instruments can help you obtain the highest yields. Remember, it is your responsibility to acquire more information before investing.

Index Funds

If you don't know anything about investing in the stock market, I recommend you start with Index Funds.

We've already seen what mutual funds are and how index funds work. I mentioned that my retirement portfolio is composed of index funds. This is because I know that over a long period of time they have grown at about 11 percent per year.

Let me share those index funds with you.

The first index fund I have chosen is the Vanguard 500 Index Fund (VFINX), because it invests in the 500 largest corporations in the United States. I have also chosen to invest in Vanguard Index Funds because they have index funds with the lowest yearly fees and no commissions.

Look for fees that are less than 1.0 percent per year. The smaller the number, the less you pay. The higher the number, the more you pay and the less your money grows.

Personally, I like someone to tell me how things work instead of trying to figure them out for myself, which is why index funds are ideal for me. Professional managers do the investing for you; you just have to understand how they work.

As I write this, I have invested in the 500 Index Fund for more than 15 years. I saw the market going down in value from March 2000 through March of 2003. During that period, I continued to invest money in the 500 Index Fund, as well as in other funds. In fact, I took advantage of the low prices over that period by buying more shares. From March 11 of 2003 through the end of that year, the 500 Index has gone up in value over 29 percent; and since 1972, it has risen 13.79 percent.

The key to investing is to invest consistently every month until you are 60, and the stock market will reward your patience.

Another fund that you can use instead of the 500 Index Fund, is the *Total Stock Market Index Fund*, which invests in the 5,000 largest companies in America. This is another fund that has grown at about 12 percent a year over a long period of time. If you are just starting out, you can use either fund to help your money grow or you can use a combination of both of them.

The second fund in which I have chosen to invest money is an index fund that follows the Russell 2000 Index. The Russell 2000 is a combination of small businesses in America, where small companies tend to go up in price faster than the big companies.

Another reason why I invest in these is because they go up and down more than large companies do. I first invest in the 500 Index Fund and diversify with the Russell 2000 Index Fund. This gives me more stability. In addition, when stocks go up, the small companies go up faster, so I take advantage of them.

The companies that represent the Russell 2000 Index have gone up in value by *12.94 since 1972.* Microsoft was a company that started small in the late '80s and was one of the fastest growing companies in America in the '90s. Today, Microsoft is one of the largest companies in the United States, but is no longer growing as fast as it did in the '90s.

I personally invest in the Vanguard Index Trust Small Cap (NAESX), which follows the Russell 2000 Index. In 2003, this fund grew at about 41.57 percent.

Finally, the third fund I invest in is an international index fund. This fund invests in companies outside the United States, all around the world. Everything that I have learned from reading investment books recommends that you invest part of your portfolio in companies outside the U.S. The reason for this is diversification. When the stock market is down in the United States, it might be up in the rest of the world and, in this way, you take advantage of that growth.

Today we have companies investing abroad and the world of business has become global, so I want to take advantage of the growth around the world. An international index fund takes care of that part of my investing without the need for me to do it individually, because I don't have the time.

The international index fund I invest in is the Vanguard Total International Stock Index Fund (VGTSX). Again, notice I invest in the Vanguard funds because their fees are the lowest in the industry of mutual funds.

Why Index Funds?

I just want to remind you why I believe index funds are a great choice to start investing money in the stock market:
1. Easy to understand
2. Less risk than other funds
3. Low yearly fees
4. No commissions
5. You invest in the U.S. economy
6. They are professionally managed
7. They have grown more than 10 percent since 1972
8. You don't have to be an expert to invest in them
9. They do better than actively managed funds
10. You achieve diversification
11. I personally sleep better investing in index funds

Before I began investing in index funds, I really didn't have an investment plan. I was just chasing and investing in the funds that were growing the fastest in a particular year. Since I wasn't analyzing these funds, all I cared about was the yield percentage. And the fund with the highest yield was the fund I invested in.

I remember when the stock market crashed in 2002. One stock I invested in was funding technology companies and had grown over 100 percent in one year. As the market crashed, this particular fund crashed too; it lost more than 80 percent of its value. Today, this fund has gone up in value, but it is still down 10 percent from the price I paid for it.

I was lucky that it was the only fund I had invested in that was not an index fund and it wasn't part of my retirement account. Every other fund in my retirement account has been invested in index funds. These went down in value too, but not like that technology fund.

You heard that many people lost a lot of money in the stock market and they lost it because they didn't have an investment plan; *they sold their stocks and stock funds because they panicked.*

I read a book that helped me a lot in formulating an investment strategy, and I recommend that everyone read it. It is *The Armchair Millionaire* by Lewis Schiff and Douglas Gerlach; their website is *armchairmillionaire.com.*

If you read this book, you will get a good education about investing. It's simple and straightforward, and will encourage you to start to invest consistently every month. The authors explain everything you need to get started by giving you strategies. And the strategies are easy to implement, just like the title suggests. I'm sure it can help you. Read it or visit their web site.

Understanding The 1/3 – 2/3 Plan

In summary, I am sharing my personal plan and it is a plan that has worked for me for the more than 20 years that I have been investing.

My plan has always been to invest 1/3 of my money in cash and real estate, and 2/3 of my money in index mutual funds. The money that I have invested in this manner is invested first inside a retirement account. However, I also have money invested outside of my retirement account in the same way. Remember, I prefer to invest first inside a retirement account because the government doesn't tax you on it while the money is growing.

Investing in the 1/3 Plan

The 1/3 plan has money in cash and in real estate. I have invested my money in the following way:

Step 1 Save "eight months" cash fund for emergencies (for a rainy day).

Step 2 Continue to save for a down payment on a house. If you have a house, you can buy a second one to rent.

Step 3 Buy a house within two years.

Step 4 If you are buying a house, prepay the mortgage.

Step 5 A goal is to reach $100,000 in cash.

Step 1

My first goal was to have the cash equal to eight months of expenses, which could be used for emergencies.

Once I had that amount, I heard a mentor say that one of his goals was to have $100,000 cash. It is a great goal to have, as you will see.

My attitude, my health and my energy improved, once I had met my goal of $100,000. When I reached this amount, I was less worried and always enthusiastic. This attitude helped me to make my business grow and, in turn, helped me to save more money.

I have this money saved in money market funds with Vanguard and, depending on how much money I have, it is invested in two or three money market funds. One fund that I used was a GNMA fund, which invests in treasury bonds. I invested in this fund because, until now, it has had a higher yield than other funds, but I also invested in Vanguard's money market fund. As you read this book, visit www.yahoo.com or www.money.com to find the money market funds that are best for you.

Step 2

Once you have saved the equivalent of eight months' worth of expenses in cash, continue to save for the *down payment* to buy a house. Remember, you already have the monthly payment to buy the house – it's the money you are paying for rent every month. Remember the example in Chapter Nine.

At first you may think, *"Where do I get the money to save $833.33 or $555.55 per month?* In Chapter Five, I explained how by saving on taxes with a part-time home-based business, you can have the money for the down payment. *"Don't focus on the problem, focus on the solution."* That is what one of my mentors told me early in my career.

How badly do you want to own a home? Focus on your goal – buying a house – and find a way to save every month for the down payment.

Step 3

Your goal should be to buy a house within two years, if you don't already own one. I have given you ideas and the tools to be able to achieve this goal.

Remember, the house will cost more in the future than it does today. I recommend that you buy a house as soon as possible.

Real estate has helped my money to grow into a million dollars. Real estate has helped others to become wealthy, too. So if wealthy people own real estate, I thought it would be good for me too. In Chapter Five, I told you how I made money through the sale of the townhouse I owned, so I urge you to buy your first house as soon as possible. Let me share the reasons why I have invested in real estate:

1. Pride of ownership
2. Better to buy than to rent (rent money disappears)
3. My money grows with real estate (inflation helps)
4. It helps me pay less in taxes to the government

5. My net worth is growing
6. With a small amount of money (a down payment of 5% or 10%), I can own a house worth $200,000 dollars
7. The value will go up in the future (inflation will help)
8. Real estate will *not cost less in the future* (inflation)
9. My children live in their own home, not in a rental
10. Better standard of living

Step 4

Once you are buying a house, you need to prepay the loan or make additional payments. In Chapter Nine, I explained that by making additional payments toward the principal, you will pay off the loan a lot faster and save on interest.

My objective has always been to not owe money to anyone. I always thought that, if I achieved this, then I could do the things I always wanted to. *Being free from the stress of worrying about money is a wonderful feeling, and you can definitely achieve this by the time you are 60.*

That's all there is to the 1/3 investment plan that I set for myself. It's easy and simple. I don't like complicated things – that's why I like it and it has worked for me.

The hardest part of making your money grow is having a plan and getting started. It's hard to start anything new, as we don't know how to do it and are afraid to make changes and risk mistakes. The easy part is making your money grow through your investments. Let's get to the easy part, investing in the plan to buy a million dollars®.

Investing in the 2/3 Plan

The money that I have invested in this part of the plan has been placed in three index mutual funds that invest in the stock market. I already explained why I invest in the market.

To reduce the risk, I invest through index funds because of their simplicity and their low annual fees. The hardest part about investing this way is choosing from among the many funds. My company of choice is The Vanguard Group, because of the variety of options they offer in index funds and the lowest annual fees on their funds compared to other companies.

Investing in the three index funds that I talked about earlier in the chapter lowers my risk when investing in the stock market and gives me the best opportunity for my money to grow into a million dollars.

Let me review these three index funds and how I invest in them:

1. The first is the Vanguard 500 Index Fund (VFINX).
2. The second is the Vanguard Index Trust Small Cap (VAESX).
3. The third is the Vanguard Total International Stock Index Fund (VGTSX).

With Vanguard, the initial investment on each fund is $3,000, but with a retirement account, only $1,000 is needed to start. The ideal is to start with equal amounts in each fund:

1. $3,000 in the 500 Index
2. $3,000 in the Index Trust Small Cap
4. $3,000 in the Total International Stock Index Fund

If you don't have the money to start with all three funds at the same time, then *start with the 500 Index*. Continue to save and then start with the *Index Trust Small Cap*, followed by the *Total International Stock Index Fund*.

Once you accomplish investing in the three funds, you can continue to save money *and invest equal amounts every month*. That's all there is to it. That's how simple my plan is to *buy a million dollars®*. Remember, I don't want my investments to worry me. I want my investments to grow my money every month and every year until I am 60 years old.

What I Know About Investing My Money

1. I know the stock market indexes have grown over 12

percent per year.
2. I know that compound interest doubles your money.
3. I know that my time limit for investing is 60 years old.
4. I know that consistency is important.
5. I know that patience is required to invest in the stock market.
6. I know that time will work in my favor.
7. I know that if I believe in my plan, it will work for me.

All I had to do for my plan to work was to get started. If I was able to teach myself to invest in the stock market, you can too! I wrote this book to make it easy for you. Just don't be afraid of getting started.

The Plan Reviewed

The 1/3 Part:
1. Eight months' worth of expense money saved for emergencies. Your goal should be $100,000.
2. Buy a house within two years.
3. Prepay your mortgage.
4. Buy a second house.

The 2/3 Part:
1. Invest equally in three index funds
   -Vanguard 500 Index Fund.
   -The Vanguard Index Trust Small Cap
   -The Vanguard International Stock Index Fund
2. Continue to invest equally in each of the funds every month.

CONCLUSION
11. THE FINISH LINE – THE TORTOISE AND THE HARE

I had been trying to get a colleague, Leticia, and her husband Juan (a successful business owner) to start saving money.

They just didn't seem to get started because of their own financial problems and because they were trying to maintain their standard of living. Finally, I told Leticia where she could save and get better rates than the bank in Mexico. But there was no branch in the city where she lived to open an account.

Juan went to Guadalajara, Mexico on a business trip and stopped by the branch to get an application. To his surprise, the rates were better than at the bank where he had a savings account. He decided to open an account and started saving, but Leticia didn't start at the same time as Juan.

I'd ask Leticia if she had started to save and her answer was always no. So every time I talked with her, I'd ask her the same thing. Have you started saving yet? Finally, two years after Juan, Leticia began to save too.

The difference was that when Juan started to save, he didn't have a plan to make his money grow, but Leticia started with my plan. She didn't understand the plan at the beginning, but, little by little, she started to understand it. All this was done over the phone, because she lives in another city.

One year later, I met with both of them to look over Leticia's investment account and this is what we discovered.

	Starting Amount	Total	Time It Took
Leticia	$1,500	$5,300	11 Months
Juan	$1,000	$5,500	3 years

In this example, both Leticia and Juan added money to their savings. The difference was that Juan just invested in a money market mutual fund and Leticia invested 1/3 of her money in a money market fund and 2/3 of her money in a stock market mutual fund.

Even though Juan started saving earlier, he didn't have a plan or pay attention to his money. Leticia started one year later with a plan and added more money to her account once a month. She learned to pay attention to her money every three weeks and was able to take advantage of the growth in the stock market in Mexico.

Juan only made about 5 percent on his money, even though he added two times more money to the mutual fund, while Leticia made about 36.3 percent on her original investment.

Leticia learned a valuable lesson. *Start to save as soon as possible, keep saving every month and take advantage of the stock market through mutual funds.* Mutual funds are a great way to make your money grow, if you don't know how to invest in individual stocks.

Leticia started to invest later than her husband, but she caught up with him because she had a savings plan. Juan started to invest earlier, but had no plan. Now he understands how important a plan is to make your money grow.

Your money will grow consistently if you have a plan. Start with your plan today.

The Future

I have learned that in investing, *the future is what really counts* and the future will be better if you have a plan today.

Not having a strategy, doing what you've always done and not trying new things are options, but not good ones. *How will your health and finances be in the future?* If you don't plan for your finances now, you'll have regrets when you are 60 years old. I repeat, the future is what counts!

I once read a book called *"If I Knew Then What I Know Now, I Would Have."* Don't let that happen to you.

Time will continue to pass. Are you going to do something so that time can help you make your money grow?

Make Mistakes

We learn by trying things and making mistakes. If you never try or make mistakes, you'll pay the price: you'll miss out on opportunities for lack of experience.

Jim Rohn, one of my mentors said, *"For things to change, you have to change. For things to get better, you have to get better."* For change to be easier, you have to totally believe in something.

If you have a mentor, it will be easier. Until you find one, use this book as a teacher and get started. This book can be the beginning of your education for making your money grow. In any case, you need to continue learning to invest so that your economic future changes for the better.

Once you find a system and a mentor, everything will be easier. He or she will help you produce the results you are looking for with your money. You only need to trust your mentor's experience, just as I did.

How do you find such a mentor with experience investing in the stock market and in real estate to guide you so you don't make mistakes? *You can only find one by looking for one. Have you started to look?*

Teach Your Children

For me, the most important thing is that I'm able to teach my children to manage money. Little by little, these concepts will make sense to them. I know the reasons why people have money problems. That's why I'm teaching my children about money, so that they don't get into trouble financially like so many people do. Triana and Kostas have begun to understand, little by little, and I know this from their comments and questions.

It's been fun teaching them because they are eager to learn and because they realize that they need money to buy the things they want. *It's easier to teach children the difference between buying things they want and the things they need.*

One of the reasons I wrote this book is so their financial lives will be easier in the future. If you apply what I've shared here, this will make a great difference.

Don't forget that children learn by example and you, the parents, are the most influential teachers in your children's lives. What are you teaching them about money?

A Final Comment

I had to learn everything in this book the hard way, and making mistakes was very important in the learning process. But if it had been easy, I don't think I would have written this book. I had to always keep learning, maintain a good attitude and continue looking for an opportunity. I didn't complain about my circumstances, but instead kept a positive outlook and tried to set a good example.

Finally, I feel everything that I've learned, all the mistakes that I made and everything I've done have prepared me to be the father that I have become.

I recommend that you be the best you can be, so you can be a good example to those who really are important in your life – your family!

Good luck.

By Greco Garcia

Books in Spanish

Book: COMPRE UN MILLON
Cost in USA $15 + tax *
Cost in México $165 pesos

Workbooks in Spanish

COMO SALIR DE LA CRISIS
Y PAGAR SUS DEUDAS
Cost in USA $8.00 + tax *
Cost in México $80 pesos

COMPRE UN MILLON
Estrategias y técnicas para hacer ganar
y hacer crecer su dinero
Cost in USA $8.00 + tax *
Cost in México $ 80 pesos

Shipping and handling in USA $4.00

*Sales tax in USA: Add 8.25% in California

**BUY
A MILLION
DOLLARS**®

Orders
Tel: (310) 827-9060 Fax: (310)827-9460
e-mail: cgreco@earthlink.net

www.buyamilliondollars.com
www.compreunmillon.com